IMAGINE

Being Excellent

Rui Da Silva

Contents

Dedication

I would like to dedicate this book to my beloved mother, Adelina,

Your unwavering spirit, boundless optimism, and infectious joy have been the bedrock of my life. You taught me to dream big, to believe in the power of imagination, and to face every challenge with a smile. Your lessons went beyond words; they were embodied in your every action, your every laugh, and your unyielding determination.

You always believed that a business was the path to true independence and fulfillment, and you nourished my ambitions with your unwavering support and love. Your reminders that nothing is impossible, if you can imagine it, have been my guiding star.

This book is a testament to your legacy and the wisdom you imparted. Thank you for being my greatest teacher, my fiercest supporter, and my most cherished inspiration.

With all my love and gratitude,

Your mentee and proud Son, Rui

To my beloved wife Julissa, whose compassion and unwavering belief in me have illuminated my path. The moment our eyes met on that dance floor, I knew I could be your present, but most of all that you were my present and my future. As we prepare to welcome our daughter, named by you in honor of my cherished mother, I am ever grateful for the love, friendship, and acceptance you bring into our lives. With your guidance and nurturing spirit, I have no doubt our daughter will become a prodigy, achieving greatness in our cosmos. Thank you for being the perfect partner and an incredible mother. Together, we will dream and shape a wondrous future.

Love Agape,

Rui

Acknowledgments

Authoring this book has been an incredible journey, and it would not have been possible without the support, guidance, and inspiration of amazing, remarkable individuals.

First and foremost, I extend my deepest gratitude to my beloved mother, Adelina. Your unwavering optimism, joy, love and wisdom have been the foundation of my life. Your teachings on the power of imagination and the importance of pursuing one's dreams have been the guiding principles behind this book.

I would like to express my heartfelt thanks to the authors who have profoundly influenced my thinking and writing. Napoleon Hill, your groundbreaking work on the power of thought and definiteness of purpose has been a cornerstone of my understanding of success. Brian Tracy, your practical insights on personal effectiveness and goal setting have shaped much of the actionable advice in this book. Dale Carnegie, your timeless lessons on building relationships and influencing others have been invaluable.

Miguel Angel Cornejo, your inspirational speeches and writings have always pushed me to strive for excellence. Og Mandino, your storytelling, and profound wisdom on the principles of success have been a source of great inspiration. Paulo Coelho, your philosophical and thought-provoking narratives have encouraged me to explore deeper meanings and spiritual dimensions in personal development.

To all the other best-selling authors and thought leaders in the personal development arena, thank you for your contributions and for paving the way with your insightful and transformative work. Your dedication to helping others achieve their fullest potential has been a beacon of light for many, including myself.

I am also immensely grateful to my family, my loved brothers Carlos, Leonel and my sister Aline, To all my friends for their endless support and encouragement. Your belief in me has been a constant source of motivation. A special thanks to my editors, designers, and everyone involved in bringing this book to life—your expertise and hard work have been instrumental.

Finally, to my followers—thank you for embarking on this journey with me. I hope this book serves as a valuable guide and inspiration as you pursue your own path to success and fulfillment.

With deep appreciation,

Rui Da Silva

About the Author

Rui Da Silva was born in Paris, France, and grew up in the Portuguese countryside, where his entrepreneurial spirit was kindled by his mother's unwavering encouragement. From a humble beginning in a small rural village, Rui started his first business at just 13 years old, turning rabbit tails and keychains into a thriving venture. This early lesson in resourcefulness and determination shaped his lifelong philosophy:

When opportunities don't exist, we create them.

At 17, Rui moved to Canada with his older brother, seeking independence and new horizons. Armed with skills honed in his upbringing—cooking, cleaning, and resilience—they navigated a foreign land. By 21, Rui had become a self-made entrepreneur and achieved a national sales record with PepsiCo, outshining seasoned professionals and setting the stage for his groundbreaking career.

As a tech visionary and the CEO of multiple award-winning companies, Rui has led innovative projects, including the first POS systems with touchscreens and multimedia kiosks for restaurants. He spearheaded cutting-edge solutions such as internet-controlled surveillance and the world's first McDonald's restaurant certified with all five integrated ISO norms in record time. His passion for innovation extends beyond technology; Rui is the author of *"Excellent Being"*, a transformative course on success principles, which has empowered thousands of mentees with a 100% satisfaction rate.

A polyglot fluent in English, Portuguese, French, and Spanish, Rui brings a global perspective to his mission of creating a better world. His life's work focuses on fostering excellence in leadership and business while advancing solutions for zero waste, clean energy, pure air, pure water, healthy and wealthy living. Rui is the founder of a Digital Marketing Agency/Cleantech and is dedicated to creating exceptional tools, such as AI-powered resources, planners, and future projects like a decentralized app and cryptocurrency, to empower individuals and businesses alike.

Rui's core belief is rooted in Luis Costa's timeless advice: *"We feed our body to survive, but if we truly want to live, we must feed our mind and soul."* His mission is to inspire individuals to self-motivate, achieve their dreams, and contribute to a harmonious world. Whether mentoring young professionals, guiding mid-career transformations, or championing ethical entrepreneurship, Rui's work is driven by a profound commitment to the well-being of humanity and the environment.

With over three decades of leadership, innovation, and mentorship, Rui Da Silva continues to transcend boundaries, empowering lives and shaping a future where science, technology, and human potential converge for the greater good.

Introduction

Imagine Being Excellent

Being Excellent is an ambitious yet rewarding pursuit. It revolves around self-improvement, a journey where one embraces personal growth and the development of essential traits. This process is neither instantaneous nor effortless; it demands a conscious effort to cultivate qualities that underpin success and fulfillment. At the heart of this journey lies the notion of incremental change. It's about recognizing the profound impact that small, deliberate shifts in mindset and behavior can have on one's life. The work delves into how such transformations often begin with a subtle shift in perspective, gradually influencing broader aspects of our existence. This exploration unfolds as we examine the traits that define excellence, offering a roadmap for those seeking both personal and professional growth.

The introduction provides a comprehensive guide to the key traits and practices that foster personal excellence. You will explore the significance of a growth mindset and its transformative potential in overcoming obstacles and achieving goals. Strategies for leveraging personal strengths effectively are examined, emphasizing self-awareness as a pivotal tool in aligning career and life objectives. The narrative extends into the realm of emotional intelligence, illustrating how virtues like resilience and empathy play vital roles in navigating challenges and building meaningful relationships. Through practical examples and insights, the chapter outlines pathways to enhance leadership qualities and emotional intelligence for young professionals, mid-career individuals, and entrepreneurs. It emphasizes the importance of adaptability and openness to feedback, encouraging a proactive stance toward life's challenges. By engaging in these ideas, you are invited to reflect on their own journeys, empowering them to take purposeful steps towards becoming truly excellent human beings.

The Power of Self-Improvement

In the transformative journey toward personal excellence, understanding and implementing strategic changes can lead to profound growth. The idea is not about making grand gestures or sweeping alterations but rather recognizing the power of small, calculated shifts in mindset and habits. These shifts, although subtle, have the potential to sweep through all areas of life, igniting personal growth and success.

Consider the concept of a growth mindset—an idea popularized by Stanford psychologist Carol Dweck. Individuals with a growth mindset believe that abilities and intelligence can be developed through dedication and hard work. This view fosters resilience, a love for learning, and a determination essential for significant accomplishments. On the other hand, a fixed mindset—the belief that abilities are static—can hinder progress. For young professionals entering the workforce, mid-career individuals seeking a fresh path, or entrepreneurs aiming to build ethical businesses, cultivating a growth mindset can be game-changing. By shifting from viewing challenges as insurmountable obstacles to seeing them as opportunities for development, you unlock new paths for progress.

Implementing strategic changes means understanding your personal strengths and leveraging them effectively. Each individual possesses unique talents and skills that, when honed and utilized, can drive personal and professional success. Self-awareness is key here. Taking time to reflect on past successes and identifying what aspects of those experiences contributed to positive outcomes can be instrumental. Yet, it goes beyond merely acknowledging these strengths; it's about optimizing them. Mid-career individuals might find themselves in roles where their strengths aren't fully leveraged. By realigning career goals and responsibilities with personal strengths, they can reignite passion and performance, leading to greater satisfaction and achievement.

For entrepreneurs, understanding team members' strengths is equally crucial. Building a business centered around the strengths of its people encourages a productive and motivated work culture. It entails creating an environment where everyone feels valued and empowered to contribute their best. When leaders recognize and nurture these strengths, it fosters an atmosphere of trust and collaboration, setting the stage for collective success.

Self-improvement is a continual process requiring ongoing dedication and adaptability. As the world evolves, so too must our approaches to growth. It's important to maintain the flexibility needed to adapt to new circumstances and challenges. The entrepreneurial landscape constantly shifts, presenting both challenges and opportunities. Entrepreneurs who remain open to changing their strategies and business models in response to market demands are often those who thrive. Similarly, young professionals entering dynamic sectors must be ready to learn continuously, acquiring new skills and knowledge to stay competitive.

Personal growth also involves being open to feedback. Constructive feedback provides invaluable insights into areas that require improvement. Humility and openness to learning from others create pathways to growth previously unseen. In practice, this might mean seeking mentorship or engaging in lifelong learning. Encouraging employees to partake in workshops or courses can enhance their skill sets and bring innovative ideas into the organization. For individual growth, investing in education that aligns with one's career objectives can yield substantial returns over time.

Moreover, embracing change demands a degree of perseverance and patience. Achieving excellence is not an overnight endeavor but a lifelong pursuit. Progress can sometimes stall, prompting feelings of frustration or doubt. Yet, understanding that setbacks are part of the journey prepares individuals to push forward with renewed resolve. Cultivating a sense of patience allows individuals to savor small victories, reinforcing a sense of accomplishment and motivating further endeavors.

The presented work illustrates how adopting a growth mindset and engaging in persistent effort leads to improvement. Dissatisfied with my results and abilities, I pursued lessons, read hundreds of books, audios and courses and shared experiences with hundreds of experts, transforming what was once a weakness into newfound amazing skills. My experience underscores the reality that improvement results from consistent effort and openness to learning, demonstrating that mindsets profoundly impact outcomes.

Loosening the grip on self-criticism can also aid personal growth. Practicing self-compassion helps maintain mental well-being and motivates individuals to pursue new challenges without fear of failure. This perspective shift from harsh self-assessment to nurturing self-reflection builds confidence and resilience, encouraging a more supportive relationship with oneself.

Defining an Excellent Being

Becoming an Excellent Human Being is a concept that resonates deeply within our shared pursuit of personal development. It involves consciously cultivating virtues like self-discipline, emotional control, resilience, empathy, and a proactive approach to life's challenges. Here, we explore how these elements combine to support personal fulfillment, success across various life domains, and ultimately, the essence of being an excellent individual.

At the core of becoming an Excellent Human Being lies the intentional practice of virtues. Self-discipline forms the backbone of virtuous living, providing the necessary framework for achieving goals and maintaining focus amid distractions. For instance, consider a young professional navigating the demands of a new job while pursuing further education. This balancing act requires disciplined time management and prioritization, enabling them to excel both in their career and personal growth endeavors. By practicing self-discipline, one builds a foundation for long-term success and stability.

Emotional control, another crucial virtue, empowers individuals to remain composed under pressure and manage stress effectively. In today's fast-paced world, emotional stability can distinguish leaders who inspire trust and confidence. Business leaders often face high-stakes decisions that impact not only their organizations but also their employees' lives. Those who exhibit emotional control are better equipped to handle tough choices with clarity and empathy, thereby fostering a positive workplace environment.

Furthermore, the transformation into an Excellent Human Being enriches one's journey toward personal fulfillment. Engaging in the practice of virtues fulfills an intrinsic motivation to grow and evolve beyond current capabilities. This sense of progress contributes to an individual's feeling of satisfaction and purpose. Take entrepreneurs like me, for example, who often embark on ventures driven by passion and innovation. Our commitment to continuous improvement and ethical business practices reflects the virtues we uphold, resulting in both personal fulfillment and broader societal contributions.

Success across various life domains also stems from this transformative process. Resilience, a defining characteristic of excellence, allows individuals to adapt and thrive even in adversity. Life inevitably presents challenges, whether in career setbacks or personal dilemmas. Resilient individuals view these obstacles as opportunities for growth rather than insurmountable barriers. This mindset fosters a robust ability to overcome difficulties and maintain momentum in pursuit of goals.

Empathy, as a key component of excellence, facilitates meaningful connections and enhances interpersonal relationships. Understanding and sharing others' feelings enable more profound communication and collaboration, essential skills in both personal and professional settings. As mid-career individuals seek renewed motivation and growth, empathy can serve as a catalyst for building supportive networks and fostering leadership qualities. It encourages openness and diversity in thought, leading to well-rounded decision-making processes.

Adopting a proactive approach to life's challenges further exemplifies the journey toward personal excellence. This attitude involves anticipating potential difficulties and taking the initiative to address them head-on. Instead of waiting for problems to arise, proactive individuals strategically plan and prepare for various scenarios. Such foresight is beneficial for aspiring leaders and entrepreneurs, who must navigate complex environments with agility and confidence. Proactivity ensures they remain ahead of the curve, seizing opportunities and mitigating risks effectively.

To inspire action, it is vital to embrace these virtues consistently in daily life. Simple yet intentional steps can significantly impact one's personal development trajectory. Start by setting clear, achievable goals aligned with your values. Develop a routine that incorporates self-reflection, encouraging ongoing assessment of your progress and areas for improvement. Cultivate relationships with mentors and peers who embody the traits you admire, learning from their experiences and insights.

Commitment to the Journey

Embarking on a journey of personal improvement is a powerful step towards becoming an excellent human being. This transformative quest requires action and a commitment to growth, but it also brings immense rewards that enhance both personal and professional aspects of life.

The first step in this journey is often the hardest—taking action. Encouraging oneself to act instills a sense of empowerment and urgency. It's vital not to delay what can be started today; procrastination only distances us from potential success and fulfillment. Start by understanding your values and set clear goals aligned with these values. Ask yourself, "What do I want to achieve?" and "Why is it important to me?" Visioning your desired future helps create a road map that guides your actions. Moreover, breaking down larger goals into manageable steps makes them less daunting and more achievable. Each step forward builds momentum, reinforcing your decision to pursue self-improvement.

As you take these steps, obstacles will undoubtedly appear. They may seem like setbacks, but reframing them as opportunities for growth transforms challenges into defining moments on your path. Consider each obstacle as a lesson, offering insights and wisdom that contribute to personal development. For instance, facing rejection in a professional setting might initially feel discouraging; however, it can prompt you to develop resilience and adaptability. By embracing these hurdles, you equip yourself with valuable skills and knowledge that prepare you for future endeavors.

Committing to self-discovery is another crucial element that leads to increased confidence and a more purposeful life. Self-discovery involves examining your strengths and weaknesses, understanding your emotions, and recognizing patterns in thoughts and behaviors. This introspective journey cultivates emotional intelligence, empowering you to manage stress, communicate effectively, and build meaningful relationships. Moreover, as you become more aware of your capabilities and aspirations, you begin to align your daily actions with your overarching purpose. This alignment fosters a sense of satisfaction and fulfillment because your efforts are directed toward meaningful objectives.

To cultivate this self-awareness, consider incorporating practices such as journaling, meditation, or seeking feedback from trusted peers. These activities offer insights into your thought processes, highlight areas for improvement, and provide clarity on your personal vision. Additionally, regularly evaluating and adjusting your goals ensures they remain relevant and challenging, keeping you engaged in your growth journey.

Another significant aspect of this journey is the courage to embrace change. Change is inherently uncomfortable, yet it is essential for growth. It requires stepping out of your comfort zone and confronting fears or limitations. However, with each leap into the unknown, you gain new experiences and perspectives that enrich your understanding of the world and yourself. Embracing change can lead to extraordinary transformations, whether it involves pursuing a new career, learning a new skill, or adopting healthier habits.

An effective way to manage change is through cultivating a network of support. Engage with communities or individuals who share similar goals and values. These connections offer encouragement, accountability, and different viewpoints that inspire continued growth. By surrounding yourself with like-minded individuals, you create a supportive environment that celebrates progress and motivates perseverance.

Moreover, gratitude plays a vital role in maintaining a positive outlook during this transformative process. Practicing gratitude shifts focus from what is lacking to appreciating what is present. It enhances well-being, reduces stress, and strengthens resilience, enabling you to navigate challenges with grace. Reflect daily on aspects of your life you are thankful for, acknowledging how they contribute to your journey of becoming an excellent human being.

Lastly, remember that this journey is ongoing. Personal growth is not a destination but a lifelong endeavor requiring dedication and adaptability. As you evolve, so too will your goals and desires. Embrace this fluidity and remain open to continuous learning and self-discovery. Keep questioning, exploring, and striving for excellence, knowing that every effort contributes to your development. Your success is the progressive realization of your dreams.

Inspiring Commitment

As this chapter draws to a close, it's essential to reflect on the transformative journey of self-improvement we have explored. We've delved into the significance of adopting a growth mindset, recognizing the power of leveraging personal strengths, and the continuous need for adaptability in an ever-changing world. These elements form the bedrock of personal excellence, driving individuals toward success across various domains of life. Whether you're a young professional striving to make your mark, a mid-career individual seeking renewed motivation, or an entrepreneur building a principled business, embracing these key traits fosters resilience and propels personal and professional growth.

Additionally, becoming an excellent human being involves cultivating virtues such as self-discipline, emotional control, and empathy. Through narrative examples and practical guidance, we've highlighted how these virtues support personal fulfillment and success. The commitment to proactive approaches and the courage to embrace change further enrich this journey, offering opportunities to grow and evolve. By engaging with like-minded communities and maintaining a positive outlook, each step forward reinforces the dedication to lifelong learning and development. This path of personal improvement is not limited to achieving goals but extends to enhancing one's ability to lead a meaningful and impactful life.

Inspired by one of my Mentors and friends, Miguel Ángel Cornejo, here's a definition of what it is to be excellent.

To Be Excellent

1. To be excellent is to do things, not looking for reasons to show that they cannot be done. Failure has a thousand excuses; success requires no explanation. The winner is always a part of the answer; the loser is always a part of the problem.

2. To be excellent is to understand that life is not something that is given to us, but that we have to create opportunities for success. Good luck comes when our opportunities meet preparation, we set up a plan and put action. It is life, my friend; as you call her, she answers: ask her for the best and she will give you the best; ask her for the worst or don't ask anything, and she will give you the worst.

3. To be excellent is to understand that with a strong discipline, it's possible to forge a winner's character. If each of us individually decides to be excellent, rest assured, there will

be one less mediocre in the world. Excellence is to think big and to start small.

4. To be excellent is to draw up a plan and achieve the desired objectives despite all circumstances. Those who want to achieve the impossible are stronger than destiny. What would the world be without dreamers?

5. To be excellent is to know when to say, "I was wrong!" and propose not to make the same mistake. There are those who accumulate wisdom and those who accumulate stupidity. Correct the wise, and they will become wiser; correct the fool, and you will cast them as enemies.

6. Being excellent is getting up every time you fail with a spirit of learning and improvement. The challenge makes the leader of Excellence, and there is no challenge without risk of failure. Assimilated failure makes the fabric, the texture of success. The winners know that it is the most certain to achieve what we desire.

7. Being excellent is to demand from ourselves the full development of our potentialities, tirelessly seeking fulfillment. The human being's universal vocation is their own and full fulfillment. Realization is the full expression of our potential, and the only way to achieve Excellence is to have the values and courage to extract the best of ourselves.

8. Being excellent is to understand that through the daily privilege of our work we can achieve realization. Let's make

every hour of our existence a masterpiece. Human beings have the option to resemble God every day through their creative talent.

9. Being excellent is to create something: a system, a position, a company, a home, a life... Human beings are in the image of God and become similar when they are creative. Excellent beings are those who are always trying to do things in a superior way. Challenge yourself and dream higher, order changes and strive tirelessly to achieve them.

10. Being excellent is exercising our freedom and being responsible for each of our actions. Free are not the ones who do what they want, but those who do what they must. Freedom is exercised by participating and committing ourselves to what we love. Freedom without commitment does not exist.

11. Being excellent is to feel offended and act against poverty, slander and injustice. Ideas will make you strong, the ideals, invincible. Excellent Beings are deeply incorporated into their community; they know part of it and understand that The ills that afflict them are the responsibility of all their members.

12. Being excellent is to lift your eyes above the earth, raise your spirit and dream of achieving the impossible. A thinker dies in a day; a dreamer lives forever. An idealistic being is like

a sun that warms, illuminates and radiates all its surroundings.

13. Being excellent is to transcend our time, bequeathing a better world to future generations. Living in excellence will make us remain forever in future generations. Beings that mark paths, that channel the achievement of ideals.

Chapter 1

Embracing the Foundation of Excellence

Excellence is not a skill to be mastered, but a mindset to be cultivated, where dedication and hard work transform potential into remarkable achievements. - **The Author**

Imagine yourself building a treehouse in your backyard. If you don't start with solid wood and a plan, you'll end up with a wobbly structure that collapses at the first gust of wind, and the only thing higher than your ambitions will be the number of splinters in your fingers!

Embracing the foundation of excellence is a journey that begins with a commitment to fundamental habits. Establishing this groundwork is not only about setting intentions but also about ensuring that each choice and action aligns with one's core values. These foundational elements serve as the bedrock upon which personal growth and achievement are built, fostering resilience and steadfastness in the face of challenges. By cultivating these basic habits, individuals create a reliable support system that guides them through both predictable routines and unforeseen obstacles, enabling them to navigate life with clarity and intent.

This chapter delves into the essential strategies for building a robust foundation for personal excellence, underscoring the role of core values in this process. You will explore how to identify and articulate their deepest beliefs, using them as guiding principles in everyday decisions. Journaling and reflective practices are highlighted as tools to gain insight into one's priorities and values. The discussion extends to practical methods for integrating these values into daily life, emphasizing the importance of setting intentions and engaging with others to reinforce commitments. Regular assessments ensure alignment with these identified values and foster continuous self-awareness and growth. Ultimately, this exploration offer you a pathway to a purposeful and authentic life, enhancing both personal fulfillment and professional success.

Identifying Core Values and Beliefs

Understanding and clarifying your core values is an essential step in building a foundation that supports personal excellence. These values act as guiding principles in decision-making and behavior, providing a steadfast anchor during times of uncertainty and creating a sense of purpose. By relying on these internal compasses, individuals can navigate challenges with greater confidence and authenticity.

Journaling or guided reflection are powerful tools for uncovering personal values. This practice allows you to explore your beliefs and priorities, gaining clarity on what truly matters when faced with choices. Through regular reflection, you align life decisions with your values, ensuring actions are true to who you are. Consider setting aside time each week to journal about experiences and decisions, noting which ones resonate most with your core values. Over time, patterns will emerge, revealing deeper insights into what drives you.

Integrating values into daily life requires intentional strategies. Begin by setting intentions that align with your values at the start of each day. For example, if kindness is a core value, consciously seek opportunities to aid others. Another strategy is sharing your values with close friends or colleagues, fostering dialogue about how these guide your actions. By vocalizing these principles, you reinforce them within yourself and make others aware of your commitments. This transparency not only strengthens your adherence to these values but also enhances consistency in decision-making, as those around you hold you accountable.

Regular assessments are crucial in maintaining alignment between your actions and identified values. They promote self-awareness and accountability, reinforcing your commitment to personal excellence. Schedule periodic reviews, perhaps monthly or quarterly, where you reflect on recent actions and decisions. Ask yourself whether they were in harmony with your core values, and where they diverged, and explore why this happened. This process encourages continuous growth and ensures you stay true to your path.

To maximize the benefits of value alignment, it's vital to embrace the reflective exercises mentioned earlier. Engage deeply with journaling practices or guided reflection sessions. These activities help identify misalignments and areas for improvement.

They also provide valuable insights into habitual behaviors that may need adjusting to better reflect your core values. As you deepen this introspective work, your understanding of self becomes more robust, enabling you to live authentically.

When integrating values into daily actions, establish a few guidelines to ensure successful implementation. Start small by choosing one or two core values to focus on initially. Create specific, achievable actions that embody these values in your everyday life. For instance, if integrity is a central value, commit to complete honesty in all interactions, however minor they may seem. By narrowing your focus, you increase the likelihood of successfully embedding these values into your routine.

Another effective guideline involves leveraging community support. Share your values with trusted individuals who can provide encouragement and feedback. Participating in groups with similar values reinforces your commitments and offers fresh perspectives on how to apply them practically. This communal approach fosters mutual accountability and shared growth.

Finally, use regular assessments as checkpoints to evaluate progress. During these evaluations, consider both successes and setbacks. Reflect on situations where you felt aligned and fulfilled, as well as those where you strayed from your values. Use these insights to adjust your strategies and strengthen your resolve. Remember, the journey towards personal excellence is ongoing, requiring perseverance and adaptability.

Building a strong foundation through core values offers resilience and direction. In moments of uncertainty or pressure, these values act as your north star, guiding your choices and actions. By investing time and effort into understanding and integrating your core values, you cultivate a life of purpose and authenticity, paving the way for personal and professional success. With dedication to this process, you not only enhance your own potential but also inspire those around you, contributing positively to your community and beyond.

Setting Clear and Achievable Goals

Goal setting is a fundamental component in achieving personal excellence, effectively transforming aspirations into actionable plans. At the heart of this transformative process lies the SMART criteria—a powerful guideline for creating effective goals. The acronym SMART stands for Specific, Measurable, Attainable, Relevant, and Time-bound, each element serving as a cornerstone to ensure goals are not only clearly defined but also realistically achievable.

Setting specific goals involves moving beyond vague statements and articulating precise objectives. For instance, rather than aiming to "improve public speaking skills," a specific goal would be "to deliver a presentation at the next monthly team meeting." This clarity provides direction and focus. Once you know exactly what you want to achieve, it becomes easier to measure progress, a crucial step in maintaining motivation. A measurable goal might involve tracking progress through regular assessments or using metrics like time spent practicing or feedback received from peers.

Goals that are attainable challenge you but remain within reach. It's essential to evaluate if the resources and support systems required are available. For example, aspiring to become proficient in a new software tool is more attainable with access to tutorials and practice environments. The relevance of a goal ensures it aligns with broader life or career aspirations, reinforcing its importance. A time-bound goal establishes a clear deadline, instilling urgency and prioritizing tasks to meet the set timeframe.

To manage larger goals and keep them from becoming overwhelming, breaking them down into smaller, manageable tasks is crucial. This approach allows for incremental achievements, offering flexibility and room for adjustments along the journey. For example, if your ultimate goal is to complete a marathon, starting with running shorter distances and gradually increasing intensity would be a sensible strategy. This method not only simplifies complex goals but also enhances adaptability, ensuring you can pivot as needed without losing sight of the overarching objective.

Visualization techniques play a pivotal role in strengthening determination, building self-belief, and clarifying desired outcomes. By picturing success vividly, individuals can enhance their emotional connection to goals, making them feel more tangible and attainable. Visualization can be practiced through mental imagery, where one imagines themselves overcoming challenges and reaching their goals, thereby boosting confidence and commitment. This mental rehearsal helps solidify the belief that the goal is achievable and worth pursuing with vigor.

Moreover, establishing accountability structures significantly enhances the likelihood of follow-through. Whether through self-accountability systems or engaging accountability partners, having someone or something to answer can drive momentum. Setting regular check-ins or deadlines encourages consistent progress and keeps motivation high. For instance, sharing your goal with a friend or joining a group with similar objectives fosters a supportive environment, creating a sense of shared responsibility and encouragement.

Creating a robust framework of accountability also involves setting up reminders and reviewing progress systematically. This could include maintaining a journal to document achievements, setbacks, and lessons learned along the way. Such reflections allow for continuous learning and improvement, helping maintain alignment with the original intent of the goal while adapting to any changes in circumstances.

Creating Daily Routines that Align with Values

Establishing daily routines is a powerful tool for translating personal values into consistent actions, ultimately driving excellence in one's life. The foundation of effective routines lies in their ability to instill discipline and provide structure, contributing significantly to enhancing overall productivity and creating stability in both personal and professional realms. By building these routines around core values, individuals ensure that their daily activities are not only purposeful but also aligned with what truly matters to them.

Routines play a critical role in fostering discipline. They act as a framework that guides behavior, making it easier to maintain focus and dedication over time. When routines are followed consistently, they create a sense of order and predictability, which can be particularly reassuring amidst the uncertainties of modern life. This structured approach minimizes decision fatigue as well, allowing individuals to conserve mental energy for more important decision-making throughout the day.

One effective way to design a routine that reflects personal values is by integrating activities that resonate with one's core beliefs and priorities. For instance, if health is a fundamental value, incorporating regular exercise or meal planning into the daily schedule becomes a priority. Similarly, for someone who values personal growth, allocating time for reading or learning new skills can be an essential part of their routine. To fully embody these values, it's crucial to regularly reflect on them and express gratitude for how they shape one's life. Setting aside time each day for reflection and gratitude allows for greater self-awareness and reinforces commitment to these values.

Incorporating time management techniques like time blocking can further enhance the efficacy of routines. Time blocking involves scheduling specific time slots for different activities, ensuring that each task gets the attention it deserves. By aligning time blocks with value-driven activities, individuals can optimize their schedules, reducing wasted time and increasing productivity. This approach not only helps in maintaining focus but also ensures that important tasks are completed efficiently, leaving room for flexibility and spontaneity within the structure.

Mindfulness practices are also invaluable when cultivating effective routines. By promoting awareness and intentionality, mindfulness enhances emotional regulation and concentration. Practices such as meditation, deep breathing, or simply taking moments to pause and be present can be seamlessly integrated into daily routines. These practices enable individuals to manage stress more effectively, maintaining a calm and focused mindset throughout the day.

Moreover, mindfulness encourages intentional living. By being more aware of their thoughts and feelings, individuals can make conscious choices about how they spend their time, rather than operating on autopilot. This heightened awareness fosters a deeper connection to personal values, enabling individuals to live in alignment with their true selves. Over time, this intentionality becomes a habit, reinforcing the positive impact of routines on one's life.

For many, achieving a balance between work and personal life remains a challenge. Routines can serve as a guiding light in navigating this balance by clearly delineating time for work-related tasks and personal endeavors. Setting boundaries within these routines—whether it's deciding to end the workday at a certain hour or dedicating weekends to family time—ensures that personal commitments receive the attention they deserve, preventing burnout and enhancing overall well-being.

Tracking progress and revising routines as needed is another aspect of ensuring their success. Regularly assessing the effectiveness of current routines allows individuals to identify areas for improvement and make necessary adjustments. Keeping a journal or using a task management system can be beneficial for this purpose, providing a tangible record of achievements and areas where changes might be needed. Flexibility is key; as circumstances and priorities evolve, so too should the routines that support them.

For young professionals entering the workforce, establishing solid routines early on can set the stage for long-term career success and personal development. These routines help in developing essential leadership qualities and emotional intelligence, critical skills in today's competitive environments. Mid-career individuals, on the other hand, might find that refining their routines revitalizes their motivation and helps overcome stagnation by promoting growth and transformation.

Entrepreneurs and aspiring leaders can leverage routines to build principled businesses grounded in ethical practices. By fostering a positive workplace culture through structured routines, they empower themselves and their teams, facilitating a productive and collaborative environment.

Understanding the Role of Motivation in Habit Formation

Embracing motivation is central to achieving and sustaining excellence, especially when it comes to developing productive habits. Recognizing the impact of motivation on habit formation can greatly enhance personal and professional growth. To truly harness this potential, it's important to distinguish between intrinsic and extrinsic motivation and understand how each influences our behavior.

Intrinsic motivation originates from within; it's driven by internal rewards such as satisfaction, interest, or enjoyment in the activity itself. Imagine a young professional who finds joy in solving complex problems at work—they're intrinsically motivated. This type of motivation often leads to more sustainable and long-lasting engagement because the individual derives inherent pleasure from the activity, not just external rewards. On the other hand, extrinsic motivation depends on external factors such as praise, money, or recognition. While it can be effective in prompting immediate action, its reliance on outside stimuli can lead to less consistent motivation over time if those rewards cease.

Strategies to engage both types of motivation can be beneficial. For instance, aligning tasks with personal interests can enhance intrinsic motivation, while setting up reward systems for achieving milestones can bolster extrinsic motivation. It's crucial to balance these motivations to avoid the 'undermining effect,' where extrinsic rewards diminish intrinsic interest. Understanding this dynamic helps in crafting environments that foster deeper engagement and persistence.

The role of motivation becomes even more evident when considering the initiation and consistency of habits. Motivation acts as the catalyst for starting new behaviors, but once established, habits themselves can reinforce the initial motivational drive. This creates a feedback loop—motivation inspires habit formation, and the success of these habits boosts motivation further. Consider an entrepreneur who begins the habit of daily exercise due to an initial health scare. As they form this habit, increased energy and clarity provide further motivation to continue exercising, showcasing the self-reinforcing nature of habits and motivation.

To cultivate a motivational mindset, celebrating small victories is essential. Acknowledging even modest achievements keeps motivation alive and provides positive reinforcement. For example, a mid-career individual aiming to improve their leadership skills might celebrate successfully handling a challenging team meeting. These celebrations don't have to be grand—a simple acknowledgment of progress suffices. Moreover, reminding oneself of the purpose and vision behind habits strengthens one's commitment. Regularly revisiting the 'why' ensures alignment with personal values and goals, providing a constant source of inspiration.

Identifying your personal 'why' is another powerful tool in cultivating a motivational mindset. This involves understanding the deeper reason behind your actions and how they contribute to your overall vision. Entrepreneurs, for instance, often have a deep-seated drive to innovate or solve societal problems. By keeping this core motivation in focus, they remain steadfast even amid challenges.

Despite best efforts, dips in motivation are inevitable. Developing resilience against these fluctuations is key to maintaining momentum. One effective strategy is creating accountability systems. For instance, sharing goals with a colleague or using productivity apps to track progress can provide that external nudge needed during low-motivation periods. Additionally, implementing self-inspiration strategies, like revisiting past successes or visualizing future achievements, can rekindle motivation. Recognizing motivation flux and accepting it as part of the process enables you to devise tailored responses rather than becoming discouraged.

Bringing It All Together

Throughout this chapter, we've explored the empowering influence of establishing a solid foundation through fundamental habits. By identifying and understanding core values, young professionals can direct their actions towards meaningful goals, ultimately crafting a life that reflects their true selves. Mid-career individuals are reminded of the importance of realigning with their values to overcome stagnation and achieve renewed motivation.

Additionally, entrepreneurs and aspiring leaders learn the value of integrating personal principles into daily routines to build robust, ethical businesses. These insights offer practical methods for anyone looking to enhance personal excellence, ensuring each step contributes to a more authentic and fulfilling journey.

By setting clear goals aligned with your values, you position yourself for long-term success. The narrative underscores how specific, measurable, attainable, relevant, and time-bound objectives guide individuals in maintaining focus and accountability. Daily routines fortified by mindfulness and intentionality further cement these values, offering consistency in an unpredictable world. Embracing both intrinsic and extrinsic motivations cultivates sustainable habits while fostering resilience through life's fluctuations. This holistic approach inspires professionals at all stages to continue growing, transforming intentions into remarkable achievements that resonate well beyond their immediate circle.

Chapter 2

The Power of Self-Discipline

Self-discipline transforms our dreams into reality, guiding our choices and actions to create the life we envision while emphasizing that true freedom lies in our ability to control ourselves being, doing and just then having. – **The Author**

Imagine yourself trying to eat just one chip from a family-sized bag: it's all fun and games until you're wrestling with your snack bowl like it owes you money. You need that self-control to avoid ending up in a cheesy, salty regret spiral!

Self-discipline is a powerful force that can propel individuals toward their desired achievements. It serves as the underpinning strength that fosters focus, dedication, and resilience in pursuing both personal and professional goals. For young professionals entering competitive job markets, mid-career individuals seeking growth, and entrepreneurs striving to lead ethically, developing self-discipline is crucial. In a world brimming with distractions, remaining committed to one's goals requires intentional effort and strategic action. This chapter explores how cultivating self-discipline through incremental victories establishes a solid foundation for success, highlighting the transformative impact of small wins on fortifying willpower and reinforcing confidence.

Throughout this chapter, you will discover the significance of building strong willpower by celebrating minor successes. These small victories not only enhance confidence but also generate momentum for tackling larger challenges. The text delves into practical strategies for establishing routines that foster discipline, emphasizing the importance of setting achievable mini-goals aligned with broader objectives. Additionally, it investigates the concept of willpower as a muscle, exploring how training it through consistent attention to small accomplishments enhances mental resilience. By acknowledging each triumph, no matter how minor, individuals can fuel their journey towards greater achievements, creating an upward spiral of motivation and drive. This chapter provides relatable insights and actionable techniques designed to equip readers with the tools to harness self-discipline effectively, ultimately paving the way for sustained personal and professional growth.

Building Strong Willpower through Small Victories

Harnessing self-discipline through the power of small victories can have a transformative impact on our confidence and ability to achieve larger goals. Nothing amplifies one's belief in their capabilities quite like incremental success. Each small triumph acts as a building block, fortifying one's sense of accomplishment and providing the necessary momentum to tackle more significant challenges.

The principle of small successes is not just about achieving micro-goals; it's about generating confidence that propels individuals forward. When young professionals or mid-career individuals encounter minor wins in their work environment, it imbibes them with a robust sense of self-assurance. This boost in confidence is critical because it diminishes feelings of self-doubt and insecurity, paving the way for aspiration and growth. As you start experiencing these small accomplishments, they create an upward spiral of motivation, making the pursuit of bigger objectives less daunting and more achievable.

Each achievement, however minor, should be celebrated. Acknowledging these wins is akin to fueling a vehicle before a long journey—each celebration adds to your reservoir of willpower. Celebrating small wins doesn't necessarily mean throwing a party every time you hit a milestone, but it could involve simple gestures of acknowledgment. Perhaps it's an internal pat on the back or a brief pause to appreciate the progress made. These celebrations serve as reminders of how far you've come and reinforce the notion that you are steadily moving toward greater goals.

The concept of willpower being analogous to a muscle is widely acknowledged. Just as with physical muscles, exerting your willpower strengthens it over time. The more you train it by focusing on small achievements, the firmer and more potent it becomes. For entrepreneurs seeking to lead with ethical practices, or professionals striving for career excellence, this understanding enables them to embrace challenges as opportunities to grow their willpower. Initially, the effort may seem substantial, but just as repeated exercise builds physical strength, consistent attention to small victories enhances mental resilience and resolve.

Creating routines based on these small successes is instrumental in fostering discipline. When mini-goals are consistently achieved, they shape habits that eventually become automatic and require minimal external motivation. Establishing such routines means incorporating small, manageable tasks into daily schedules, ensuring they align with larger objectives. For example, if an aspiring leader aims to enhance communication skills, daily practices such as reading a chapter from a leadership book or engaging in short public speaking exercises can gradually build competence and confidence. Over time, these actions become ingrained, leading to improved skills without conscious effort—a phenomenon known as automaticity.

For young professionals entering the workforce or entrepreneurs building their businesses, setting mini-goals provides clarity and focus. An effective guideline is to identify specific, attainable targets that align with broader ambitions. By breaking down substantial goals into smaller, actionable components, individuals can avoid feeling overwhelmed and remain enthusiastic about their progress. Just as an artist sketches preliminary outlines before painting, mini-goals offer a framework upon which grand visions can be constructed.

Tracking progress is another integral aspect of cultivating the habit of celebrating small victories. Keeping a journal or using digital tools to record accomplishments helps visualize growth over time. This practice serves as a motivational tool, providing tangible evidence of improvement and reinforcing the positive effects of small wins. Moreover, it facilitates reflection, allowing individuals to reassess strategies and make necessary adjustments to stay on course.

Incorporating these small successes into daily routines is vital for establishing discipline. For instance, setting aside five minutes each morning for planning the day or reviewing priorities can enhance productivity and structure throughout the day. As these small actions compound, they create a disciplined rhythm that supports large-scale achievements.

Implementing Strategies to Overcome Procrastination

Procrastination can feel like a steep wall in the path of productivity. For young professionals, mid-career individuals, and entrepreneurs, identifying habits that lead to procrastination is essential for overcoming it effectively. The first step is to pinpoint the specific moments or tasks where procrastination tends to set in. This could be during mundane tasks or complex assignments that seem overwhelming. Understanding these triggers enables you to develop strategies tailored to circumvent them.

Consider John, a mid-career manager who finds himself delaying monthly report submissions because the task seems repetitive and uninspiring. By recognizing this tendency, John can implement changes such as tackling the report earlier in his work cycle or breaking it into smaller segments, focusing on one section each day. By addressing these specific moments, he not only completes his task on time but also reduces stress associated with last-minute rushes.

The Pomodoro Technique serves as another powerful tool against procrastination. This method involves working in short, focused intervals, typically 25 minutes, followed by a five-minute break. Such timed work sessions keep distractions at bay and maintain energy levels, ensuring sustained productivity throughout the day. Using this technique, Sarah, an aspiring entrepreneur, schedules her writing tasks into Pomodoro sessions, enabling her to manage her workload efficiently while avoiding burnout.

For those seeking more engagement, establishing rewards for task completion provides significant motivation. Whether it's a small treat after finishing a project segment or indulging in a favorite activity at the day's end, rewards create a positive reinforcement loop. This tactic transforms otherwise daunting tasks into achievements worth celebrating. Consider David, a graphic designer who promises himself a weekend movie night once his weekly projects are completed. This motivational boost encourages him to diligently pursue deadlines without feeling overwhelmed.

Visualizing the long-term costs of inaction is another effective approach. Often, we fail to act due to a lack of immediate consequences. However, reflecting on the future implications of our delay can heighten urgency and prompt swift action. Emma, a team leader, regularly reminds herself of how postponed tasks could snowball into larger challenges affecting her team's morale and performance. By imagining these outcomes, she finds renewed commitment to tackling tasks promptly.

To mitigate procrastination, it might be useful to employ a guideline focused on identifying procrastination triggers: list down activities and contexts where procrastination creeps in, recognize patterns, and consciously implement alternate strategies to tackle them. Additionally, the Pomodoro Technique benefits from structured guidelines; select a task, set a timer for 25 minutes, focus solely on that task, note distractions if they occur, and take a five-minute break—a process that repeats to help maintain momentum.

Setting up a consequence and reward system can also have practical guidelines. Define clear tasks and corresponding rewards, ensuring they are meaningful enough to motivate action yet achievable to avoid adding pressure. Alongside, consider penalties for unmet goals, such as contributing to a social cause or missing out on a leisure activity. This creates accountability paired with intrinsic motivation.

In understanding these techniques, it becomes evident that a blend of awareness, structured breaks, incentive systems, and visualization can form a robust front against procrastination. By harnessing these tactics, individuals across various stages of their careers can enhance focus, bolster commitment, and ultimately drive success through disciplined action.

In essence, combating procrastination is about implementing conscious changes. For example, Liam, an accountant, realized that mornings were his most productive times, yet he often spent them answering emails that could wait. Realigning his schedule to prioritize complex tasks during peak hours allowed Liam to make better use of his natural rhythms, thereby minimizing periods of procrastination. Such self-awareness and strategic adjustments not only help realize immediate objectives but also pave the way for sustained growth and achievement.

The Time Management Significance and Prioritization

In the quest for success, self-discipline stands as a cornerstone. A crucial aspect of developing self-discipline is mastering time management and prioritization. The ability to efficiently allocate time and prioritize tasks not only leads to higher productivity but also builds the focus and commitment necessary for long-term achievement.

One proven method for effective prioritization is the Eisenhower Matrix. This powerful decision-making tool helps individuals differentiate between what is urgent and what truly matters. By categorizing tasks into four quadrants—urgent and important, important but not urgent, urgent but not important, and neither urgent nor important—it becomes clear where one's immediate attention should be directed and which tasks can wait or even be eliminated entirely. Understanding this distinction is vital; it allows individuals to manage their time effectively by focusing efforts on tasks that align with their overall goals, rather than getting bogged down by less significant demands. Using the Eisenhower Matrix, one can create a balanced approach to task management that prevents unnecessary stress and inefficiency.

Once priorities are established, planning becomes the next step in building self-discipline. Effective planning involves anticipating potential obstacles and allocating the necessary resources and time to overcome them. Recognizing the challenges that may arise during a project allows for proactive strategies to mitigate risks and maintain progress. Planning should start with defining the end goal and breaking it down into manageable steps. By doing so, each component becomes part of a comprehensive strategy that moves closer to the final objective. Furthermore, planning is not just about scheduling tasks but also about setting realistic timelines and ensuring that resources such as materials, manpower, and finances are allocated appropriately.

The use of digital tools like calendar apps and task lists can significantly enhance time management efficiency. These tools provide visibility and accountability towards deadlines, serving as constant reminders of duties and helping to prevent procrastination. Calendar applications allow users to schedule tasks with specific start and end times, while task lists offer a clear overview of daily objectives. By integrating these tools into one's routine, it's easier to track progress, make timely adjustments, and ensure that no task is overlooked. Moreover, these digital solutions often come with features such as notifications and recurring task settings, reinforcing consistency and aiding in the development of self-discipline.

As life circumstances and commitments evolve, so too should one's planning processes. It's important to remain flexible and adjust plans to accommodate new priorities or unexpected changes. Long-term success isn't merely about sticking rigidly to a schedule but about adapting strategies to meet current demands without losing sight of overarching goals. Regular evaluations of progress and plan effectiveness can lead to adjustments that better serve evolving needs. This adaptability ensures sustained momentum and reduces the likelihood of falling into complacency or becoming overwhelmed. A dynamic planning process acknowledges that change is inevitable and encourages resilience and resourcefulness in tackling new challenges.

The path to cultivating self-discipline through time management and prioritization is paved with intention and action. By distinguishing between urgency and importance using the Eisenhower Matrix, individuals can direct their focus toward meaningful tasks that contribute to personal and professional growth. Thoughtful planning anticipates challenges and prepares pathways to surmount them, while digital tools keep tasks visible and deadlines in clear view. Adjusting plans to align with shifting priorities ensures that discipline remains steadfast in the face of change.

By embracing these practices, young professionals, mid-career individuals, and entrepreneurs alike can harness the power of self-discipline. For those entering the workforce, these skills lend an edge in establishing credibility and achieving early career milestones. For those seeking growth and transformation, time management becomes a vehicle for rekindling motivation and pursuing new opportunities with vigor. Entrepreneurs and aspiring leaders gain from structuring efforts toward ethical practices and team empowerment, fostering a workplace culture that thrives on discipline and dedication.

Utilizing Accountability for Sustained Discipline

Accountability plays a crucial role in maintaining self-discipline, acting as the backbone that supports perseverance and commitment. One effective way to harness accountability is by teaming up with accountability partners. These partnerships foster mutual motivation and commitment, creating an environment where both parties are invested in each other's success. When individuals collaborate on their objectives, they share resources, provide support during challenging times, and celebrate successes together. This shared journey enhances the determination to remain disciplined, as the presence of a partner provides encouragement and develops a sense of responsibility toward achieving goals.

In addition to accountability partnerships, making public commitments can significantly bolster self-discipline. By publicly declaring intentions or goals, individuals create a form of social pressure that drives them to fulfill their commitments. This pressure arises from the natural human desire to maintain integrity and avoid the embarrassment of reneging on promises. Public declarations can be made through various platforms, such as social media or by sharing goals with friends and colleagues. The fear of letting others down often provides an extra push, helping individuals stay disciplined even when faced with obstacles or dwindling motivation.

Routine evaluations also play an integral role in maintaining focus and addressing challenges collaboratively. Regular check-ins offer opportunities for self-reflection, allowing individuals to assess their progress and identify areas needing improvement. During these evaluations, people can gather feedback from their accountability partners or peers, ensuring that any issues are addressed promptly. Collaborative efforts to solve problems not only reinforce discipline but also nurture creativity and innovation, as diverse perspectives are brought into play. Establishing a routine for these evaluations helps maintain momentum and keeps individuals aligned with their goals, fostering sustained dedication over time.

Another valuable tool for enhancing accountability and self-discipline is visual tracking. By visually representing progress, whether through charts, graphs, or goal trackers, individuals gain heightened awareness of their commitments and achievements. This tangible representation serves as a constant reminder of where they stand regarding their objectives. Visual tracking tools can range from simple handwritten lists to sophisticated digital applications that provide real-time updates on progress. The consistent visibility of one's journey reinforces the importance of staying on track and motivates individuals to maintain discipline as they witness incremental advances.

To effectively implement these strategies, it is beneficial to establish guidelines for partnerships and evaluations. For instance, when setting up an accountability partnership, partners should agree on specific roles and expectations. This agreement might include how often they will communicate, what forms of support they will offer each other, and how they will handle setbacks. Clarity in these arrangements enhances the efficacy of the partnership, ensuring that both parties remain committed and mutually beneficial.

For routine evaluations, it is essential to set clear benchmarks and schedules. Deciding upfront how frequently these evaluations will occur and what metrics will be assessed can streamline the process. Regularity in evaluations fosters consistency in self-assessment and ensures that discipline remains a focal point amidst the inevitable distractions of daily life. A guideline here could involve setting quarterly reviews where individuals reflect on their achievements, reassess their strategies, and make necessary adjustments to stay aligned with their long-term goals.

When utilizing visual tracking, the key is simplicity and relevance. Tools or methods chosen should be easy to understand and directly related to the goals at hand. Over-complicated systems may become burdensome and counterproductive. Instead, opt for straightforward methods that clearly indicate progress and motivate continued effort. Whether it's a physical vision board or a digital dashboard, the primary aim should be to keep individuals engaged and aware of their journey toward self-discipline.

Finally, it's important to integrate these accountability methods within a broader framework of personal development. Establishing a personal development plan can serve as a roadmap, outlining the steps needed to achieve goals and ensuring accountability through defined actions. This structured approach allows for breaking down larger goals into manageable tasks, promoting a sense of achievement and forward momentum. By adhering to a well-defined plan, individuals take ownership of their growth journey, holding themselves accountable for the necessary actions required to succeed.

Bringing It All Together

As we wrap up this chapter, it's essential to recognize the transformative power of self-discipline nurtured through small victories. The journey showcased how these incremental successes build confidence and fortify willpower step by step. By celebrating each minor achievement, we're not only validating our progress but also fueling our ambition to tackle larger challenges. This approach encourages young professionals and mid-career individuals alike to establish mini-goals that align with broader aspirations. Such targeted efforts can sharpen focus and commitment, crucial traits needed to excel and thrive in any field.

For entrepreneurs and aspiring leaders, embracing small victories offers a blueprint for ethical leadership and effective team management. These achievements instill discipline and automaticity in pursuing objectives, transforming daunting tasks into structured routines manageable over time. As we've explored, disciplined actions are rooted in consistent, intentional practices that lead to personal and professional growth. With these insights, readers are equipped to harness self-discipline as a catalyst for success, fostering environments where individuals and teams can flourish together.

Chapter 3

Enhancing Emotional Intelligence

Empower yourself to navigate your emotions and understand others, you will develop deeper connections and build stronger relationships that foster both personal and professional growth. Unless you continue to remember it, there's nothing wrong with being wrong sometimes. **- The Author**

Imagine yourself learning to dance at a wedding. Sure, you might stumble over your own feet initially, but once you get the rhythm of recognizing your own feelings and those of others, you'll be the star of the dance floor instead of that one person who just sways awkwardly by the punch bowl!

Enhancing emotional intelligence plays a crucial role in navigating the complexities of interpersonal relationships and developing internal resilience. By understanding our emotions better, we equip ourselves with the tools needed to engage meaningfully with others and confront life's challenges with poise and confidence. Whether it's in personal or professional settings, a heightened sense of emotional awareness allows individuals to respond thoughtfully rather than react impulsively. This chapter will guide readers through a journey of self-discovery, focusing on identifying personal emotional triggers and how they impact daily interactions.

Throughout this chapter, you will learn various techniques to deepen your emotional understanding and improve your interactions with others. We begin by exploring the importance of recognizing and accurately naming emotions, paving the way for greater clarity and reduced misunderstandings in communication. You'll discover practical strategies such as journaling to track emotional patterns and the benefits it brings for personal growth. Additionally, the chapter delves into the significance of identifying recurring emotional responses, which can be pivotal in resolving conflicts and enhancing collaboration. By the end of this exploration, you'll gain insights into the integral role that emotional intelligence plays in fostering effective communication and building strong, resilient connections in your professional and personal life.

Recognizing and Understanding Your Emotions

Understanding and mastering emotional intelligence is key to enhancing interpersonal relationships and building internal resilience. To achieve this, it is critical that individuals first gain insight into their own emotional states. This awareness helps in deciphering how emotions influence daily actions and interactions. Emotional intelligence, when developed, provides a clear pathway for personal growth and effective communication.

One essential task in understanding emotional intelligence is recognizing one's personal triggers. These are events or situations that evoke strong emotional responses, which can often lead to impulsive reactions if not managed correctly. By identifying these triggers, individuals are better equipped to handle situations strategically. For instance, if loud criticisms trigger anger, knowing this beforehand allows an individual to prepare mentally and manage their reaction more constructively. This proactive approach to managing emotions means that rather than reacting defensively, one can engage in calm, strategic communication. This mindfulness can reduce misunderstandings and clear paths for productive dialogue.

Furthermore, journaling emerges as a powerful tool for organizing thoughts and feelings. Keeping a journal may seem old-fashioned, but it offers remarkable benefits for self-reflection and personal growth. Writing down daily experiences and emotions enables individuals to spot patterns in their behaviors and emotional responses. For example, by documenting instances that led to stress or joy, one can better understand what drives their emotional highs and lows. Over time, these insights provide a systematic way to analyze personal growth and facilitate the development of coping strategies. When looking back at past entries, individuals get the chance to reflect on progress, learning from past experiences and thus evolving their emotional intelligence.

Recognizing recurring emotional patterns plays a significant role in conflict resolution. Patterns reveal themselves through repeated emotional responses to similar situations. If someone consistently feels frustrated during team meetings, this pattern indicates an underlying issue that must be addressed. By noticing these patterns, individuals can adjust their behavior accordingly to avoid future conflicts. Perhaps changing the way contributions are voiced or altering expectations can transform tense interactions into collaborative opportunities. By consciously adjusting such patterns, individuals hone their ability to navigate conflicts with poise and efficacy.

Equally important is the practice of naming emotions accurately. Too often, people might describe feeling "bad" without delving deeper into whether they mean sad, anxious, or overwhelmed. Properly labeling emotions facilitates control over them and leads to healthier expressions. When individuals identify exactly what they're feeling, it demystifies those emotions and takes away some of their power. Instead of becoming engulfed by a vague sense of discomfort, naming emotions aids in approaching situations with composure, ultimately reducing anxiety. This clarity enhances interpersonal interactions because when people properly articulate their feelings, it encourages transparency and fosters mutual understanding. A conversation that starts with acknowledging "I feel frustrated" is far less likely to spiral into a quarrel compared to vague declarations like "I'm just upset."

All these elements point towards a broader purpose: helping you develop the skills to navigate their emotional landscapes with insight and balance. Understanding these concepts empowers individuals to manage their emotions effectively, enabling them to interact more productively with others. Through recognizing triggers, engaging in regular journaling, identifying emotional patterns, and naming emotions explicitly, individuals build a foundation for personal and professional success. These practices serve as guidelines for anyone seeking to enhance their emotional intelligence, which is vital in thriving within increasingly complex social environments.

Developing emotional intelligence isn't about suppressing emotions; rather, it's about cultivating an awareness that leads to mindful expression. In doing so, young professionals, mid-career individuals, and entrepreneurs alike can establish robust careers and create positive workplace cultures. As individuals continue to refine their understanding of emotional states and their impacts, they will find themselves better equipped to face challenges with empathy, strategic communication, and resilience.

By incorporating these techniques into daily routines, individuals expand their emotional toolbox, equipping themselves to deal with diverse interactions and situations. Discovering personal triggers allows for planning and adapting responses suited to each unique context. Journaling assists in sorting through complex emotions and finding clarity amidst confusion. Identifying patterns provides a roadmap to steer clear of repetitive pitfalls, and proper naming of emotions enriches communication with authenticity and reduced tension.

Practicing Empathy in Daily Interactions

Empathy stands at the core of emotional intelligence, playing a vital role in nurturing strong relationships and fostering understanding across diverse perspectives. In an increasingly interconnected world, developing empathy is crucial for young professionals, mid-career individuals, and entrepreneurs who aspire to excel in their fields by cultivating meaningful connections.

Active listening forms the foundation of empathy, providing a channel through which individuals can truly understand one another. This skill involves engaging fully with the speaker, maintaining eye contact, and using verbal and non-verbal cues such as nodding or brief affirmations like "I see" or "I understand." These actions demonstrate that you are present and attentive, creating a space where the speaker feels valued and heard. Such engagement validates the speaker's emotions, helping to foster mutual respect and significantly reduce potential conflicts. Active listening combined with empathy improves relationships between couples, families, and coworkers by allowing genuine human connection to flourish.

Taking the time to walk in someone else's shoes is another critical aspect of empathy, offering a pathway to broaden our perspectives. When we attempt to understand the experiences and feelings of others, we cultivate patience and improve our ability to solve problems effectively. Picture a team facing a challenging project deadline: a manager who empathizes with the pressures facing each team member can devise strategies that accommodate individual stressors, leading to enhanced morale and productivity. By actively seeking to understand various viewpoints, we not only strengthen our relationships but also evolve into more effective problem-solvers.

The recognition of both verbal and non-verbal cues further solidifies empathetic communication, guiding us towards more thoughtful responses. Non-verbal signals such as facial expressions, tone of voice, and body language often convey emotions more potently than words alone. Ignoring these cues can lead to misunderstandings, while acknowledging them can deepen our bonds with others. For instance, noticing a colleague's subtle sigh or tense posture during a meeting can prompt you to offer support or a break, showing that you value their well-being. Empathetic leaders who tune into these signals create environments where team members feel safe and understood, paving the way for open and collaborative interactions.

Responding with compassion is a powerful practice that builds trust and fosters an environment conducive to growth and support. When we respond to others with kindness and understanding, we communicate that they are not alone in their struggles. This creates a sense of belonging and security, encouraging openness and collaboration. Consider a scenario where a coworker shares a personal difficulty affecting their performance. By expressing empathy through simple statements like, "That sounds tough; I'm here if you need anything," you reinforce trust and solidarity, enabling them to navigate challenges with greater ease.

To effectively implement these principles, guidelines can be useful. For active listening techniques, focus on three key practices: maintaining eye contact, reflecting on what was said by paraphrasing, and asking clarifying questions. This structured approach ensures that the speaker feels acknowledged and understood. Similarly, embracing the mindset of walking in someone else's shoes requires a conscious effort to suspend judgement and nurture curiosity about their perspective. Practicing patience and openness to differing opinions enriches our understanding and deepens our empathetic capacity.

Recognizing verbal and non-verbal cues necessitates attentiveness. Begin by observing body language and facial expressions closely, as these often reveal unspoken emotions. Pay attention to changes in tone or volume, which may signal underlying feelings. Acknowledging these cues when responding reinforces the message that you genuinely care about the person's experience.

Lastly, responding with compassion can be guided by adopting a mindset focused on kindness and support. Whether in personal conversations or professional settings, always prioritize empathy by envisioning yourself in the other person's situation. This mindset shift naturally leads to compassionate responses that build trust and nurture open, supportive environments.

Mastering Emotional Regulation Techniques

In today's fast-paced world, controlling emotional responses is crucial for effective decision-making. As individuals look to strengthen their personal and professional lives, developing strategies to manage emotions becomes essential. Here's a closer look at several methods that can help in this regard.

One effective strategy is the practice of mindfulness. Mindfulness involves being present and fully engaged with the current moment without being overly reactive or overwhelmed by what's happening around us. This technique helps reduce emotional escalations and enhances focus, which is vital for making clear and thoughtful decisions. By practicing mindfulness, young professionals and leaders can ensure they respond thoughtfully rather than impulsively when faced with challenging situations. Engaging in mindfulness exercises such as meditation or simple daily awareness practices can increase one's ability to remain calm and centered. Research suggests that mindfulness not only improves attention but also aids in regulating negative emotions, contributing to better executive function.

Breathing techniques are another powerful tool for managing stress and stabilizing emotions, especially in heated moments. When emotions run high, physiological changes occur in the body, often leading to increased heart rates and tension. Learning specific breathing exercises—such as deep breathing, breath counting, or alternate nostril breathing—can provide immediate relief. These techniques activate the body's parasympathetic nervous system, promoting relaxation and helping to bring clarity and composure back into decision-making processes. For mid-career professionals experiencing stagnation, breathing techniques offer an easily accessible way to regain control over emotions and reset mentally during stressful times.

Equally important is cognitive reappraisal, a method that involves changing the way we interpret various situations. By reframing our thoughts, we can alter our emotional responses, turning potentially negative experiences into opportunities for learning and growth. This form of cognitive flexibility fosters resilience and enhances creative problem-solving skills, which are invaluable in both personal and professional settings. For example, if a project doesn't go as planned, instead of viewing it as a failure, one might see it as a chance to learn new skills or explore different perspectives. Studies confirm that cognitive reappraisal is linked to experiencing more positive emotions daily, which supports long-term well-being and satisfaction.

Setting emotional boundaries is another critical aspect of managing emotional responses effectively. Emotional boundaries involve knowing where your emotions end and another's begin, enabling you to protect your well-being while maintaining healthy relationships. This clarity helps in balancing personal needs with external demands, allowing for more controlled and deliberate reactions. By establishing these boundaries, individuals can avoid unnecessary emotional entanglements that may cloud judgment or lead to stress. Entrepreneurs and aspiring leaders, in particular, can benefit from setting clear emotional boundaries to maintain productive workplace cultures while ensuring their teams feel supported and empowered.

Incorporating these strategies into everyday life requires practice and dedication. However, the benefits of honing these skills are significant and far-reaching. By consistently practicing mindfulness, engaging in regular breathing exercises, employing cognitive reappraisal techniques, and clearly defining emotional boundaries, individuals at all stages of their careers can enhance their emotional intelligence. This improved emotional management not only facilitates better decision-making but also strengthens interpersonal relationships and builds internal resilience.

For those embarking on their professional journeys, mastering these techniques early on can serve as a foundation for future success. Meanwhile, mid-career individuals seeking transformation will find that these strategies can reignite motivation and enhance their leadership qualities. Finally, entrepreneurs aiming to build ethical and effective businesses will discover that managing emotions adeptly fosters a positive environment conducive to growth and innovation.

Using Emotional Awareness for Better Decision-Making

Understanding emotions is pivotal in the process of making thoughtful decisions, particularly for individuals navigating complex personal and professional landscapes. By recognizing the influence of emotions, decision-makers can gain clarity on their motivations and align their choices with rational objectives.

Acknowledging the impact of emotions serves as a foundational step toward rational and unbiased decision-making. Emotions often operate in the background, subtly guiding our thoughts and actions. Recognizing how they shape our motivations allows us to question whether our desires stem from logical considerations or momentary feelings. For instance, a young professional might feel inclined to accept a job offer because of the excitement associated with it, rather than weighing the long-term benefits objectively. By acknowledging this emotional impact, an individual can realign their focus toward evaluating factual aspects such as career growth opportunities, compensation, and work-life balance, leading to more balanced and informed decisions.

Balancing intuition and logic further enhances decision commitment and confidence by incorporating emotional insights. Intuition, often described as a gut feeling, can sometimes conflict with logical reasoning. However, combining these two elements enriches the decision-making process. Entrepreneurs, for example, may rely on intuition when entering new markets. While data-driven analyses provide valuable insights into market trends and consumer behavior, intuitive understanding can guide entrepreneurial ventures towards unique opportunities that statistical models might overlook. This synergy between intuition and logic not only increases the individual's confidence in their decisions but also fosters a deeper commitment to seeing those decisions through.

Reflecting on past decisions offers a window into growth patterns and helps avoid repeated mistakes through emotional learning. The ability to look back and analyze previous choices enables individuals to identify successful strategies and recognize where they could have acted differently. Mid-career individuals facing stagnation may benefit from this reflective process. By examining previous career moves or business decisions, they can discern patterns of success or failure tied to specific emotional responses. Over time, this introspection fosters personal growth and allows for adjustments based on learned experiences, ultimately reducing the likelihood of making similar errors in the future.

To aid in this reflection, creating a structured approach is beneficial. One guideline is to maintain a decision journal, noting the emotions experienced during each significant choice. This practice not only records decisions but also documents the emotional states accompanying them. Over time, reviewing these entries reveals patterns and provides insights into which emotional cues led to favorable outcomes and which did not. Such reflections can become powerful tools for personal development and more informed decision-making.

Visualization techniques also play a crucial role in foreseeing emotional outcomes, aligning decisions with core values, and minimizing future regret. Visualizing potential scenarios and their associated emotional impacts helps individuals assess whether their decisions are congruent with their long-term goals and values. For young professionals and entrepreneurs focused on ethical practices, visualizations can ensure that every decision reflects integrity and aligns with their vision for the future.

One practical guideline is to engage in guided visualization exercises. Before making a decisive call, such as launching a new product or changing careers, imagine the possible outcomes and how each would make you feel. Consider the pride and satisfaction of success versus the disappointment of unmet expectations. This exercise helps clarify what truly matters and aids in making choices that reduce regret while boosting overall contentment with one's path.

Bringing It All Together

This chapter has delved into the profound influence of developing emotional intelligence on enhancing interpersonal relationships and building internal resilience. It highlights the importance of being aware of one's own emotions, recognizing personal triggers, and understanding how these emotions can shape daily interactions. The techniques discussed, such as journaling and identifying emotional patterns, offer practical methods for individuals to navigate their emotional landscapes with greater insight and composure. By mastering these skills, you are empowered to engage in more meaningful and mindful communication, both personally and professionally. This awareness not only aids in conflict resolution but also supports a clearer expression of emotions, thus fostering stronger connections with others.

The journey toward refining emotional intelligence is about embracing one's emotional experiences rather than suppressing them. With strategies like accurate emotion naming and the proactive management of emotional responses, individuals across different career stages—whether young professionals, mid-career individuals, or entrepreneurs—can enhance their personal growth and leadership qualities. These practices provide a solid foundation for navigating complex social environments, ensuring that individuals are better prepared to face challenges with empathy and resilience. As readers incorporate these approaches into their daily lives, they expand their emotional toolkit, equipping themselves to handle diverse situations with greater confidence and effectiveness.

Chapter 4

Cultivating a Growth Mindset

Our thoughts shape our reality, and with perseverance in the face of challenges, we transform obstacles into opportunities for growth and innovation. **- The Author**

Imagine yourself tending to a garden. If you treat failures like weeds and learning opportunities like sunshine, you'll soon find yourself with a flourishing jungle of possibilities—just watch out for those pesky squirrels looking to steal your nuts of wisdom!

Cultivating a growth mindset involves embracing challenges and viewing them as opportunities for development. This mindset is not just about thriving in favorable circumstances; it's about navigating adversities and using them as a foundation for resilience. By shifting our perspective to see obstacles as essential elements of personal and professional growth, we open ourselves up to continual learning and innovation. Whether encountering setbacks or facing new experiences, adopting a growth mindset empowers individuals to explore uncharted territories with confidence and creativity. This chapter delves into the transformative power of this mindset and how it enables enduring success through adaptability and perseverance.

In exploring the concept of cultivating a growth mindset, readers will gain valuable insights into several key areas. The narrative journey begins with understanding how reframing failure can serve as a catalyst for creativity rather than a deterrent. It continues by examining the role of seeking discomfort as a way to expand one's capabilities and adapt to change. Furthermore, the chapter highlights the importance of curiosity as a tool for deep problem-solving and innovative thinking. Additionally, celebrating small wins is emphasized as an essential practice for sustaining motivation and building self-confidence. Through these discussions, the chapter provides practical strategies for adopting a growth-oriented approach that encourages resilience, continuous improvement, and the courage to embrace lifelong learning.

Embracing Challenges as Opportunities

Viewing challenges as opportunities is a transformative mindset that capitalizes on adversity to build resilience. By shifting how we approach setbacks and difficulties, we empower ourselves to thrive in ever-changing environments. This subpoint explores how reframing failure, seeking discomfort, using curiosity as a tool, and celebrating small wins contribute to developing this resilient mindset.

Let's begin with the concept of reframing failure. Instead of viewing failure as a conclusion, consider it a steppingstone toward improvement. This perspective fosters an environment where creativity can flourish, unencumbered by fear. When you see failure as part of the learning process, each setback becomes a chance to grow. For example, Thomas Edison famously saw his unsuccessful attempts to create the light bulb not as failures but as education in what didn't work. By adopting this viewpoint, you allow innovation to take root and evolve through trial and error. Thus, embracing failure becomes essential in generating new ideas and pushing boundaries.

Next, seeking discomfort intentionally pushes you out of your comfort zone, accelerating growth and adaptability. Growth rarely occurs within the familiar; it's the unfamiliar territories that challenge us to adapt and innovate. Consider athletes who train under unusual conditions to enhance their endurance and agility. Such practices prepare them for unexpected circumstances during competitions. Similarly, stepping into discomfort can mean taking on roles you're less familiar with, tackling projects outside your expertise, or simply trying something new regularly. Through these actions, you cultivate flexibility and versatility, traits invaluable in rapidly changing environments.

Curiosity, often underestimated, serves as a powerful driver for overcoming obstacles. It involves exploring questions and engaging deeply with problems rather than skimming the surface for quick solutions. Curiosity leads to deeper understanding and innovative problem-solving. When faced with a challenge, a curious mind asks why and seeks alternative perspectives and approaches. For instance, businesses that encourage curiosity among employees often see increased problem-solving capabilities and innovations in products or services. This proactive approach steers individuals toward continual learning, transforming obstacles into opportunities for discovery and advancement.

Moreover, celebrating small wins plays a crucial role in maintaining motivation and reinforcing abilities. In any endeavor, it's important to acknowledge incremental progress instead of solely focusing on large achievements. Recognizing and celebrating small victories helps sustain motivation over time, reminding us of our capabilities and boosting morale. For instance, breaking down a significant project into smaller tasks and celebrating the completion of each step can keep you motivated. These celebrations need not be grand but should validate the effort and dedication put forth. As motivation increases, so does confidence, driving continued perseverance.

Learning from Criticism and Feedback

Embracing feedback is essential for continuous improvement, as it fosters personal growth and development in both professional and personal contexts. By treating feedback as a valuable tool rather than a personal insult, individuals can cultivate openness and enhance their emotional intelligence. Constructive feedback, when viewed positively, becomes an opportunity to learn and grow. It's an indicator of areas that need attention, not a judgment of one's abilities or worth. Understanding this can lead to significant improvements in how we handle challenges, perform tasks, and ultimately succeed.

Constructive feedback serves as the bedrock for developing openness and emotional intelligence. In today's fast-paced world, where adaptability is key, being receptive to feedback allows individuals to adjust their actions and strategies for better outcomes. This approach requires a shift in perspective, seeing feedback as an external insight aimed at nurturing one's potential. It has been noted in various studies, such as those highlighted by Daniel Goleman's research in "What Makes a Leader," that accepting constructive criticism enhances emotional intelligence, which in turn contributes positively to personal and professional success. Emotional intelligence encompasses skills like self-awareness, empathy, and social skills—all crucial attributes for effective leadership and collaboration.

Actionable insights gained from feedback help pinpoint specific areas for measurable progress and skill development. When feedback is detailed and focused on tangible aspects, it offers clear direction on what should be improved. For instance, a young professional might receive feedback about presentation skills—notes about clarity, engaging storytelling, or improved visuals can serve as actionable insights. Armed with this information, they can work on specific areas rather than feeling overwhelmed by general criticism. This targeted approach not only facilitates skill enhancement but also encourages a sense of achievement as individuals witness noticeable progress. The journey of continuous learning becomes more structured, enabling individuals to set realistic goals and benchmarks.

Building resilience is another vital outcome of embracing feedback. Accepting criticism gracefully involves understanding that setbacks are part of the growth process, and that neither success nor failure is permanent. Instead of viewing criticism as a blow to self-esteem, resilient individuals use it as a steppingstone for future endeavors. This ability to maintain motivation and quickly recover from setbacks is vital in high-pressure environments where challenges are frequent. Developing resilience through feedback not only strengthens character but also keeps the drive alive, pushing individuals towards achieving their aspirations despite obstacles.

Engaging in self-reflection using feedback is crucial for gaining a deeper understanding of one's strengths, weaknesses, and goals. Reflective practices allow individuals to internalize feedback, leading to enhanced self-awareness. By examining the reasons behind a particular piece of feedback, individuals can connect it to broader patterns in their behavior or performance. This introspection aids in forming a clearer view of what needs attention and how small changes can make a considerable difference. Through reflection, individuals can discern between feedback that aligns with their personal goals and values, and feedback that may not be relevant, thereby preventing unnecessary stress.

Creating an environment where feedback is welcomed and actively sought out can substantially enrich personal and organizational culture. In workplaces, fostering such an atmosphere cultivates trust and transparency, encouraging team members to feel valued and part of the group's success story. Feedback-rich cultures are characterized by open communication and collaboration, where individuals are motivated to share ideas and innovate without fear of negative repercussions. Harvard Business Publishing highlights that high-trust environments significantly reduce stress and increase engagement, showcasing that a feedback-centered approach yields substantial benefits.

To harness the full potential of feedback, it's imperative to establish systems that promote effective communication. Training leaders and employees to deliver and receive feedback constructively is crucial. Active listening, empathy, and practical communication are skills that can be honed through workshops and seminars, enabling people to articulate their observations respectfully and productively. Additionally, utilizing technology, such as online platforms for anonymous feedback or regular check-ins, streamlines the feedback process and provides data-driven insights for informed decision-making.

Follow-up actions based on feedback are equally essential. Feedback should not just be collected but acted upon to enable continuous improvement. Implementing necessary changes and communicating the outcomes reinforces the value of feedback and shows a commitment to progress. This ongoing cycle of feedback and action creates a dynamic, evolving environment where individuals and teams thrive.

Persisting Despite Setbacks

In today's fast-paced world, persistence stands as a cornerstone for success, particularly when facing inevitable challenges. Persistence is not merely about enduring tough times; it's about developing the mindset to view obstacles as steppingstones toward achievement. A crucial component in cultivating this mindset is understanding the Resilience Framework, which suggests that setbacks are integral parts of our success narratives. This framework encourages individuals to embrace adversity as a necessary element of their journey, guided by a clear vision of their goals.

The Resilience Framework advocates for viewing challenges not as roadblocks but as opportunities to grow stronger. Take the story of Thomas Edison, who famously failed hundreds of times before successfully inventing the light bulb. His perseverance typifies the resilience needed to overcome repeated failures without losing sight of his ultimate goal. Individuals who adopt this mindset can reframe their struggles into critical learning experiences, essential for crafting success stories punctuated by moments of triumph over adversity.

Moreover, adopting a long-term perspective is instrumental in maintaining focus on the end goal. This perspective fosters patience and consistency, virtues that are crucial for sustaining effort over time. In the corporate realm, many successful leaders have navigated prolonged periods of uncertainty by keeping their eyes on the horizon. Achieving long-term success requires setting realistic timelines, identifying incremental milestones, and celebrating each small victory along the way. By focusing on stretched goals rather than immediate gratification, one develops the tenacity to persevere, even when progress seems laborious.

Within this journey, emotional regulation plays a pivotal role. Emotional regulation refers to the ability to manage and respond to emotional experiences with mindful awareness. It helps decrease impulsivity during setbacks, enabling wiser decision-making and reinforcing perseverance. Without effective emotional regulation, emotions can cloud judgment, leading to rash decisions that might derail progress. For instance, entrepreneurs often face high-stakes situations that require calm composure and calculated responses. Through practices such as mindfulness and stress reduction techniques, individuals can learn to navigate their emotions effectively, transforming potential triggers into motivators for sustained effort.

Support systems also prove invaluable in the pursuit of long-term success. These systems can include accountability partners or mentors who provide guidance and encouragement. The presence of supportive relationships offers both psychological and practical benefits. An example is the mentoring relationship between business magnate Warren Buffett and his long-time friend and partner Charlie Munger. Their mutual respect and shared wisdom serve as a continuous source of inspiration and strategic insight, enabling them to persistently pursue their objectives.

Accountability partners serve another critical function: they hold individuals to their commitments, encouraging perseverance when self-motivation wanes. They offer constructive feedback, helping to fine-tune strategies and maintain alignment with overarching goals. A structured support system thus acts as a crucial buffer against discouragement, providing the moral and intellectual support necessary to sustain long-term pursuits.

When building a resilient pursuit plan, incorporating Constructive Feedback and Actionable Insights is incredibly beneficial. A guideline here could involve regularly seeking input from peers or mentors to pinpoint specific skills that need development. Constructive feedback, when viewed as a valuable resource rather than a personal attack, can promote openness and humility. This approach helps individuals identify areas where adjustments can lead to significant improvements. Meanwhile, actionable insights derived from feedback provide clear, measurable points for personal growth, ensuring that persistence is continuously aligned with improvement.

Crafting an environment conducive to persistence involves weaving these elements together. Viewing setbacks as part of a larger success narrative helps develop resilience. Adopting a long-term perspective empowers individuals to keep their aspirations within reach, no matter the distance. Emotional regulation transforms potential hindrances into opportunities for calculated moves, while robust support systems offer guidance and accountability.

Celebrating Effort Over Talent

Valuing effort is a vital component of fostering intrinsic motivation and promoting continuous improvement. This subpoint delves into the significance of acknowledging and rewarding efforts to develop a growth-focused mindset and nurture environments conducive to learning and achievement.

A growth-focused mindset places emphasis on the recognition of hard work over innate ability, encouraging individuals to persist in the face of challenges. When people understand that their skills and intelligence can be developed through dedication and effort, they are more likely to persevere and ultimately achieve empowerment. This mindset fosters an attitude where setbacks are viewed as opportunities for growth rather than insurmountable obstacles. The belief that one's efforts lead to tangible improvement inspires individuals to push their limits, try new approaches, and adapt to varying circumstances.

In various professional settings, encouraging a culture of effort involves acknowledging each team member's contributions, regardless of the outcome. This recognition fosters productivity, satisfaction, and collaboration among colleagues, creating an environment where everyone feels valued and motivated to contribute their best. Effort-based recognition transforms a workplace into a supportive space where employees are invested in each other's success. By focusing on the process rather than solely on results, organizations can cultivate a sense of belonging and shared purpose, enhancing overall morale and efficiency.

Implementing strategies for celebration is another key aspect of promoting a culture of effort. Recognition systems that reward consistent hard work not only increase morale but also set the standard for what is valued within an organization. Celebrating milestones, both big and small, reinforces the importance of perseverance and encourages ongoing participation from all members. These celebrations might include public acknowledgment during meetings, commemorative awards, or even simple gestures of appreciation like personalized notes. Such practices create a positive feedback loop, motivating individuals to continue putting forth their best effort and inspiring others to follow suit.

Internal gratification is essential for sustained motivation, stemming from the joy found in the process itself and valuing progress over perfection. Intrinsically motivated individuals derive satisfaction from mastering tasks and overcoming challenges, finding fulfillment beyond external rewards. This focus on internal gratification helps maintain enthusiasm and commitment, especially when extrinsic rewards are not immediately apparent. Acknowledging personal achievements and recognizing incremental improvements, no matter how small, helps build self-esteem and reinforces a sense of accomplishment that fuels continued growth.

Intrinsic motivation is inherently powerful because it aligns closely with self-determination, driving behavior towards self-improvement and adaptation. When individuals experience the satisfaction inherent in activities themselves, they engage more deeply and consistently with their pursuits. This engagement often leads to discovering novel strategies and developing competencies that enable them to tackle unforeseen challenges effectively. In professional contexts, this adaptability translates into a capacity for lifelong learning and innovation, ensuring individuals remain competitive and relevant in ever-evolving industries. Recognizing the value of effort underscores the idea that learning and development do not occur solely through talent but through persistent endeavor.

Furthermore, growth-focused mindsets have been demonstrated to improve academic performance across various subject areas. In educational settings, emphasizing effort over inherent ability has resulted in significant improvements in student outcomes, particularly in subjects perceived as challenging. Students with a growth mindset approach difficult problems with resilience, understanding that intelligence can grow with dedicated effort. Instilling this belief in young professionals entering the workforce equips them to navigate complex landscapes with confidence and determination.

Promoting effort within teams and organizations involves guiding individuals to recognize the pivotal role their actions play in achieving results. Providing autonomy and clear expectations enables team members to take ownership of their tasks, increasing engagement and accountability. Leaders who model a growth-focused mindset inspire others through their example, embedding values of perseverance and effort within the organizational culture. By fostering environments where effort is acknowledged and celebrated, leaders lay the groundwork for a collective commitment to excellence and continuous improvement.

Ultimately, valuing effort cultivates an ecosystem where individuals are empowered to realize their potential by embracing learning as an ongoing journey. Encouraging a focus on effort empowers individuals to see challenges as steppingstones and failures as invaluable lessons. This perspective nurtures resilience, creativity, and innovation, unlocking possibilities for personal and professional growth. Whether for young professionals, mid-career individuals, or entrepreneurs, recognizing the significance of effort as a cornerstone of success ensures a pathway toward enduring achievement and fulfillment.

Closing Remarks

In this chapter, we have explored the significance of adopting a growth mindset in promoting resilience and lifelong learning. By embracing challenges as opportunities, individuals can shift their perspective on failures, viewing them as steppingstones rather than dead ends. This mindset fosters creativity and innovation, encouraging people to step out of their comfort zones and seek discomfort as a path to personal and professional growth. Through curiosity, one can delve deeper into problems, transforming obstacles into opportunities for discovery and improvement. Celebrating small wins along the way helps maintain motivation and builds confidence, reinforcing the ability to persevere through challenging times.

We also considered the impact of feedback on continuous development. By treating feedback as an opportunity for learning rather than a personal affront, it becomes a valuable tool for enhancing emotional intelligence and fostering openness. Understanding that setbacks are temporary, resilient individuals use criticism constructively, aiding self-reflection and personal insight. Building environments where feedback is valued enriches organizational culture, promoting trust and collaboration among team members. Persistence, emotional regulation, and strong support systems further contribute to long-term success, empowering individuals to turn challenges into stories of triumph. Ultimately, valuing effort over talent creates a growth-focused mindset, enabling people to realize their potential and adapt to ever-changing landscapes.

Chapter 5

Overcoming Self-Doubt and Fear

Over 95% of the things we worry about either never come to pass or, if they do, teach us valuable lessons along the way. A seemingly small fear can easily transform into a trauma if allowed to linger unchecked in our minds. It's important to remember that in moments of panic, our ability to think clearly is compromised. So, when in doubt, embrace action and take that leap—often the first step is all it takes to conquer uncertainty!"- **The Author**

Imagine yourself peering at a bed bug under a microscope. This tiny parasite, nearly invisible to the naked eye, sits magnified at 1000x, transforming its minuscule form into a daunting creature on the glass stage. As you study it, your mind begins to play tricks, inflating its size until it seems as large as a monster lurking in the shadows. Now, take a step back, open both eyes wide, and take a deep breath. In that moment of clarity, you realize it was merely an illusion; the bed bug is still small, and it's your imagination that turned it into something fearsome!

Overcoming self-doubt and fear is an endeavor that can open numerous doors to personal growth and new opportunities. The challenge lies in recognizing these feelings as natural, yet surmountable, obstacles rather than insurmountable barriers. Self-doubt, often birthed from comparing oneself to others, can foster insecurity and limit potential. Our modern world, deeply influenced by social media, frequently exacerbates these feelings, presenting idealized versions of life that can make the viewer feel inadequate. However, this doesn't have to be a permanent state of mind. Understanding and confronting these experiences not only enhances self-awareness but also creates pathways for transformation and empowerment.

This chapter delves into the intricate process of identifying the sources of self-doubt and fear, offering readers insights on how to confront these feelings head-on. Examining how past experiences influence self-perception, it guides individuals to view failures as steppingstones rather than setbacks. Additionally, the role of one's environment in shaping confidence is explored, highlighting the importance of nurturing supportive relationships and surroundings. Journaling emerges as a recommended practice, providing a structured way to navigate emotions and track personal progress over time. You will discover practical approaches to reframe insecurities and utilize them as catalysts for growth, ultimately fostering a mindset geared toward success and resilience.

Identifying Sources of Self-Doubt and Fear

Recognizing and understanding the roots of self-doubt and fear are vital steps in overcoming these barriers. By addressing underlying causes, individuals can unlock new levels of personal growth. Self-doubt often originates from comparing oneself to others. This comparison fosters insecurity by highlighting perceived deficiencies. In today's social media-driven culture, it's easy to fall into the trap of comparing one's behind-the-scenes life with other's highlight reels. Such comparisons are rooted in an illusion, as they don't account for the struggles and vulnerabilities that everyone faces. To curb this insecurity, self-reflection is essential. Through introspection, individuals can recognize their unique strengths and accept that no one is infallible.

Analyzing past experiences offers another avenue for addressing self-doubt. Negative episodes, such as failures or rejections, can result in distorted self-perceptions. These events often create a narrative of inadequacy, overshadowing future potential with memories of past setbacks. By examining these triggers, individuals can differentiate between historical failures and future possibilities. Each setback becomes an opportunity to learn rather than a prophecy of repeated mistakes. Transforming these narratives requires conscious effort and patience, enabling individuals to look beyond past failures and embrace opportunities for success.

Furthermore, one's environment plays a significant role in shaping confidence and self-esteem. External influences, including people and surroundings, impact how individuals perceive themselves. A supportive environment nurtures confidence, whereas negative influences can erode self-worth. If surrounded by people who belittle or undermine, individuals may doubt their abilities and worth. It becomes vital to reassess these influences and make conscious decisions to alter them. Surrounding oneself with positive, encouraging individuals who celebrate successes and offer constructive feedback can significantly enhance self-confidence. This shift supports personal development and fosters an environment conducive to overcoming self-doubt and fear.

Journaling stands out as a powerful tool for navigating these internal challenges. Keeping a journal allows individuals to map out fears and doubts, providing clarity and insight into emotional landscapes. Writing down thoughts and feelings helps externalize internal conflicts, making them easier to analyze and address. The act of journaling encourages mindfulness, allowing individuals to acknowledge their fears without judgment. This process promotes a deeper understanding of personal triggers and patterns, facilitating the development of actionable pathways toward overcoming self-doubt. Journals also serve as a record of progress, illustrating personal growth over time and reinforcing the positive changes achieved through introspection and reflection.

Understanding that insecurities are deeply connected to comparative thinking can be liberating. By acknowledging the root of insecurity, individuals can shift focus away from others and back onto personal growth. This redirection is not about ignoring one's deficiencies but about recognizing them as part of a shared human experience. Everyone has areas for growth, and embracing this fact allows individuals to engage in self-improvement without harsh self-criticism. The journey toward self-awareness begins with accepting imperfections and using them as catalysts for transformation.

To further illustrate the importance of analyzing past experiences, consider how successful individuals often use failure as a steppingstone rather than a barrier. Famous figures frequently recount stories of failure as pivotal moments that redirected their paths toward eventual success. Such stories underscore the concept that failure is not indicative of inadequacy but a natural part of the learning process. By viewing failures as temporary and educational, individuals can separate past experiences from future ambitions, instilling a renewed sense of capability and confidence.

The environment's influence is equally critical, often dictating one's level of self-assurance. For example, professional environments that prioritize constructive feedback and recognition can foster employee growth and innovation. Conversely, toxic workplaces breed self-doubt, stifling creativity and progress. Reassessing one's surroundings and making deliberate choices to inhabit spaces that uplift can significantly impact personal and professional trajectories. Creating a network of supportive peers and mentors who encourage risk-taking, and resilience can radically improve self-image and confidence.

Journaling provides a structured means to navigate these complex realities. By consistently documenting personal thoughts, individuals gain perspective on recurring themes in their lives. Journals can help identify moments when self-doubt was overcome and detail strategies that can be employed again in similar situations. They serve as a guidebook filled with insights unique to each individual's experience. Furthermore, reviewing past journal entries reinforces the narrative of growth and resilience, reminding individuals of their ability to navigate challenges successfully.

Utilizing Positive Affirmations and Visualization

Positive affirmations and visualization are powerful tools in the journey of overcoming self-doubt. These methods serve not only to bolster confidence but also to transform one's outlook on life by building resilience and reducing anxiety.

Daily affirmations play a crucial role in reshaping negative thought patterns. By consistently articulating positive statements, individuals can challenge and change their internal dialogue. For instance, replacing thoughts like "I can't handle this" with affirmations such as "I am capable and prepared to face challenges" can significantly alter one's mindset over time. This shift fosters a more optimistic outlook, which has been shown to reduce anxiety and enhance resilience. The repetitive nature of affirmations helps ingrain these positive beliefs into one's subconscious, effectively rewiring the brain to focus on strengths rather than weaknesses.

Visualization techniques complement affirmations by allowing individuals to mentally rehearse success. By vividly imagining achieving their goals, people can psychologically counteract self-doubt. Visualization boosts motivation and reinforces personal belief in their ability to realize desired outcomes. For example, athletes often use this technique to enhance their performance by visualizing themselves excelling in their sport. Similarly, professionals can imagine themselves confidently navigating challenging situations at work, thereby enhancing their self-assurance when encountering similar scenarios in reality.

Incorporating mood or vision boards with affirmations creates tangible reminders of an individual's aspirations. These boards act as physical manifestations of personal goals, serving as motivational tools that reinforce the pursuit of success. When coupled with daily affirmations, they provide a comprehensive approach to maintaining focus on what truly matters. For instance, a vision board filled with images and quotes that represent a career goal can remind someone of their ambitions, making it easier to stay motivated and combat feelings of self-doubt.

While positivity is important, authenticity remains key. Avoid using generic stock affirmations, as their impact is limited compared to personalized messages. Crafting affirmations that resonate deeply with personal values ensures greater effectiveness. They should reflect genuine aspirations and be grounded in realistic terms to prevent discouragement or unrealistic expectations. This not only makes them more relatable but also ensures a lasting impression on one's psyche. Statements like "I am learning new skills every day" can be more effective than overly ambitious claims disconnected from one's current reality.

Routine practices involving affirmations and visualization must align with personal values to provide long-term impacts on self-image. It is essential to integrate these exercises into daily life in a manner consistent with one's core beliefs and objectives. By doing so, individuals can foster a sustained positive shift in how they view themselves and their abilities. This alignment helps maintain authenticity in the affirmation process, grounding them in meaningful personal truths rather than superficial assertions.

Developing a habit of regular practice amplifies the benefits of these techniques. Setting aside time each day for affirmations and visualization helps embed them into one's routine, increasing their potency. Practitioners can begin with short sessions and gradually increase the duration as they become more accustomed to the practice. Consider beginning each day with a few minutes dedicated to reciting affirmations or spending some time visualizing the day's goals during a lunch break. Over time, these practices become second nature, seamlessly integrating positivity into daily life.

These proactive approaches are not confined solely to individual pursuits; they also extend to fostering better relationships in professional settings. Entrepreneurs and leaders can employ these strategies to enhance teamwork and cultivate a positive workplace culture. By encouraging employees to adopt similar practices, they can inspire a collective boost in morale and productivity. This shared commitment to personal and professional growth cultivates an environment where everyone feels empowered to contribute their best efforts.

The power of affirmations and visualization lies in their ability to create a mental framework conducive to success. By visualizing desired outcomes and affirming their capacity to achieve them, individuals build a strong foundation for personal development. These techniques empower people to navigate the challenges of self-doubt and fear with grace and confidence, ultimately unlocking their potential for growth.

Taking Calculated Risks to Build Confidence

Stepping out of your comfort zone is an essential step toward building resilience and courage. For young professionals, mid-career individuals, and entrepreneurs, embracing discomfort can lead to significant personal growth. Truly understanding the delicate dance between risk-taking and rewards is key in this journey. It's not about taking reckless risks but learning to identify calculated ones that hold the potential for growth. Calculated risks are informed, deliberate decisions made after considering potential outcomes and aligning with personal goals.

Imagine a scenario where you're offered a challenging project at work. Accepting it might seem daunting, but the potential rewards could be immense. The key lies in evaluating the risks and crafting a plan that navigates obstacles while seizing opportunities. This ability to analyze and choose wisely is crucial in transitioning from fear to empowerment.

Gradual exposure to discomfort can yield transformative results. Consider a person who is terrified of public speaking. Starting with a small audience and progressively increasing the audience size allows them to build confidence incrementally. With each step, the comfort zone expands, resulting in newfound self-assurance. This cumulative effect doesn't happen overnight but rather through consistent practice. Over time, what was originally intimidating becomes second nature.

Failures can be daunting, yet adopting a mindset that views setbacks as learning experiences is crucial. A growth mindset encourages individuals to embrace challenges, see effort as a path to mastery, and learn from criticism. By shifting the perception of failure from an endpoint to a steppingstone, individuals become more resilient. The story of Thomas Edison is a testament to this philosophy. When asked about his experiments that didn't work, he famously said he found thousands of ways not to make a light bulb. This relentless pursuit eventually led to success, highlighting the power of persistence and learning from mistakes.

Building a support system is pivotal when venturing beyond familiar boundaries. Accountability groups, mentors, or supportive friends offer guidance and encouragement during risky endeavors. Just as athletes rely on coaches for support, having someone to share fears and successes with can significantly alleviate the stress associated with risk-taking. These alliances foster motivation, reduce anxiety, and create a safety net that cushions potential falls.

The notion of expanding the comfort zone aligns with the concept of self-agency. By frequently stepping outside familiar confines, individuals gain deeper insights into themselves and develop a stronger grip on steering their lives. This journey also introduces them to new experiences, broadening their horizons and potentially uncovering new passions or interests. Interaction with diverse situations widens their perspective, allowing them to appreciate varied viewpoints and cultivate empathy, a vital trait for both personal development and leadership.

It's worth noting that humans are naturally inclined to avoid perceived threats due to survival instincts. However, distinguishing between actual dangers and opportunities for growth is fundamental. Regularly assessing areas where life feels too comfortable can provide insights into why certain aspirations remain unfulfilled. For instance, if a dream job requires skills outside one's current expertise, identifying this gap can initiate a journey of skill acquisition, moving one step closer to achieving professional aspirations.

However, it's essential to balance periods of intense growth with moments of rest. Just as sustained physical exertion without breaks leads to exhaustion, pushing oneself relentlessly can result in burnout. Drawing parallels with physical training, it's wise to allocate specific times for stepping out of the comfort zone, ensuring there are intervals for recuperation. This rhythm ensures continuous growth while maintaining mental and emotional well-being.

Reframing stress as a catalyst rather than a hindrance also aids in this transition. Recognizing stress as eustress, or positive stress, empowers individuals to leverage it constructively. This energy can propel them to perform under pressure, whether delivering a compelling presentation or spearheading a new business venture. Embracing stress in this manner transforms it into a powerful ally in the journey from fear to empowerment.

Acknowledging neuroplasticity, the brain's ability to adapt and change, further bolsters the courage to venture into unfamiliar territories. Understanding that the brain can rewire itself based on experiences encourages individuals to take that initial leap away from comfort. Each endeavor acts as a stimulus for growth, proving that capabilities are not fixed but evolve with every new challenge faced.

Reflecting on Past Successes for Encouragement

In moments of self-doubt, reminding oneself of past achievements can serve as a powerful antidote. This subpoint encourages keeping a record of these successes to build confidence and resilience.

Creating a success journal is an effective way to document accomplishments. Whether it's landing a first job or completing a challenging project, chronicling these events reinforces a positive self-image. During times of negativity, a quick glance through the journal can remind individuals of their capabilities, serving as a much-needed boost to their self-esteem. An entry could recount a well-executed presentation, noting how the preparation paid off and what skills were utilized. Such reflections not only uplift during hard times but also highlight the progress made over time.

Recognizing and celebrating small accomplishments are equally essential. Success is not always about grand achievements; it's often built on minor victories that pave the way for larger ones. Acknowledging these moments fosters a sense of competence and resilience. For example, consistently meeting daily goals like organizing one's workspace or successfully communicating with a team member should be noted. These seemingly minor tasks contribute to a greater feeling of control and achievement, nurturing a mindset geared towards future successes.

Visual stimuli can also play a crucial role in reinforcing motivation. Photos, certificates, or even mementos from events where success was achieved act as anchors in uncertain times. They serve as tangible reminders of personal growth and achievement. Displaying these items at home or in the workplace can provide continuous motivation and confidence reinforcement. Such visual cues help maintain focus and determination, especially when self-doubt creeps in.

Mentoring others provides another powerful avenue to combat self-doubt. Sharing personal journeys and experiences allows individuals to rediscover their strengths and talents. Teaching or guiding someone else not only reinforces one's own knowledge and skills but also fosters growth through shared experiences. Mentors often find themselves reaffirming their confidence by seeing their advice and support make a tangible difference in someone's life. The dual growth in this mentoring relationship helps both mentor and mentee develop a deeper understanding of their potential and capabilities.

Bringing It All Together

In this chapter, we explored how identifying and confronting self-doubt and fear can lead to remarkable personal growth. We identified the roots of these emotions, such as the comparisons often fueled by social media, and analyzed past experiences that might have contributed to self-doubt. By transforming our narratives about failures into opportunities for learning, individuals stand a stronger chance of unlocking their potential. The environment around us also plays a pivotal role in shaping self-esteem, with supportive surroundings fostering confidence. Practices like journaling offer a tangible way to navigate doubts, helping individuals recognize patterns and record progress. These approaches serve as pathways to overcoming insecurities, shifting focus from external comparisons to internal growth.

Furthermore, we delved into the power of positive affirmations and visualization as tools to combat self-doubt. By consistently practicing these methods, individuals can reshape their internal dialogues and visualize success. Coupled with calculated risk-taking, these practices can transform fear into empowerment, encouraging individuals to step out of their comfort zones while expanding their horizons. Reflecting on past successes provides another source of encouragement, reinforcing self-belief and resilience through documented achievements. By acknowledging small victories and mentoring others, individuals can further strengthen their confidence. As readers implement these strategies, they can pave the way for personal development, cultivating an enduring sense of confidence and capability.

Chapter 6

The Art of Effective Communication

It is not the moments in which we breathe that mark our existence, but rather those that take our breath away. - **The Author**

Imagine yourself playing a game of telephone at a family reunion. One moment, you're whispering that Aunt Linda makes the best lasagna, and the next, Uncle Joe thinks you said she's running for president! The key is to ensure your message doesn't get lost in translation!

Effective communication is a fundamental skill that impacts every aspect of personal and professional life. It is not simply about exchanging information but about understanding the emotions and intentions behind words. Mastering the art of effective communication can lead to more rewarding relationships, enhanced trust, and greater influence over others. At its core, effective communication involves a blend of speaking, listening, and interpreting non-verbal cues that convey messages beyond spoken language. This chapter delves into the nuances of this skill, offering tools and techniques essential for building influence and leadership in diverse environments. By honing these skills, individuals can better navigate complex interactions, reduce misunderstandings, and create lasting connections with those around them.

In order to achieve excellence in communication, several key components will be explored throughout the chapter. Beginning with active listening, readers will learn how to fully engage with speakers, fostering an environment of trust and understanding. The chapter will then address common barriers to effective communication, such as distractions and biases, and provide strategies to overcome them. You will also gain insights into crafting clear and concise messages, ensuring your thoughts are communicated with precision to avoid misinterpretations. Additionally, the importance of non-verbal signals will be highlighted, emphasizing how body language can enhance or undermine verbal communication. Through exercises and practical examples, this chapter aims to equip you with actionable skills, enabling them to transform your communication approach and achieve more meaningful interactions in both personal and professional spheres.

Developing Active Listening Techniques

Active listening is an essential communication skill that can significantly enhance personal and professional interactions. Unlike merely hearing, active listening demands full engagement with the speaker, aiming to cultivate a meaningful connection and provide clarity in conversations. This skill involves consciously directing your attention to the speaker, both mentally and emotionally, to sincerely understand their message. Active listening in itself is an art form—it's about being present and creating a safe space where the speaker feels valued and respected.

One of the key components of active listening is providing reflective responses, which play a critical role in validating and affirming the speaker's emotions. By reflecting back on what you've heard, you not only confirm your understanding but also demonstrate empathy and concern for the speaker's needs. For instance, if a colleague shares a challenging situation at work, replying with something like, "It sounds like that situation was really stressful for you," confirms to them that their feelings are acknowledged. This build-up of trust can strengthen relationships, making collaboration more effective.

However, several barriers can impede effective communication, obstructing the flow of active listening. Distractions are one such hurdle. In our fast-paced, technology-driven world, it is easy to become sidetracked by external stimuli—such as mobile devices or competing noises—or internal distractions like wandering thoughts and assumptions. Additionally, preconceived notions and biases can distort our perception of the speaker's words, leading to misunderstandings. For example, if you assume a peer always complains, you might tune out vital details when they discuss issues, missing important information. Overcoming these barriers requires conscious effort and awareness.

To enhance active listening skills, regular self-reflection is crucial. Self-reflection allows you to examine and assess your listening habits, identifying areas for improvement. It encourages you to consider questions like: Am I genuinely attentive when others speak? Do I often interrupt or interject my opinions prematurely? Through honest reflection, you can recognize patterns in your listening behavior and develop strategies to amend them. Practicing mindfulness techniques, such as focused breathing, can help center your attention during conversations, while setting aside time after interactions to reflect on your listening approach can yield insights into how you process information and respond to others' cues.

Guided by these principles, several techniques can be employed to enhance active listening. First and foremost, giving the speaker your complete attention is vital. This means maintaining eye contact, using open body language, and nodding or providing verbal affirmations where appropriate. These simple non-verbal cues show the speaker that you are fully engaged in the dialogue. Furthermore, asking open-ended questions encourages further discussion and demonstrates your interest in exploring the speaker's perspective. Questions like, "Can you tell me more about that?" invite deeper conversation and clarify points that may have been initially vague.

Another technique is paraphrasing and summarizing what the speaker has said. This doesn't mean repeating verbatim but rather conveying the essence of their message in your own words. It ensures that you've accurately understood their points and gives them the opportunity to correct any misinterpretations. For instance, saying, "So what you're saying is…" followed by a concise recap of their message shows attentiveness and confirms understanding. Additionally, withholding judgment and refraining from immediate advice-giving cultivates a supportive environment, allowing the speaker to express themselves freely without fear of criticism.

Despite its importance, mastering active listening requires persistent effort and dedication. It is not an innate ability but a skill honed through practice and application. Just as an athlete trains to improve performance, so too must individuals commit to developing their listening prowess. This includes incorporating active listening techniques in everyday interactions, observing how others respond, and adjusting approaches based on feedback received.

Crafting Clear and Concise Messages

Effective communication is the bedrock of successful interaction, allowing for clear understanding and diminished chances of misinterpretation. In a world where the speed and complexity of information exchange are ever-increasing, mastering this skill becomes crucial for anyone aiming to influence and achieve leadership in their field.

Clear communication acts as a cornerstone for minimizing misunderstandings and resolving conflicts, thus enhancing efficiency in interpersonal and professional settings. When a message is conveyed with precision, it diminishes the likelihood of misinterpretation, which can lead to unnecessary disputes. This clarity ensures that time and energy are not wasted on resolving conflicts that could have been avoided with careful communication.

One common barrier to clear communication is the use of jargon. While technical or specialized language may seem convenient among experts within a particular field, it often alienates those who are not familiar with such terminology. Communicating effectively involves stripping away jargon to ensure the core message is accessible to everyone in the conversation. Imagine explaining a complex technological concept to someone with no background in the field; using plain language not only makes the topic understandable but also widens the audience who can engage with the subject matter.

To elucidate an idea effectively, structuring thoughts logically before communicating them is vital. Logical structuring involves organizing ideas coherently, so they follow a natural progression that makes sense to the listener or reader. Whether delivering a presentation, writing an email, or engaging in a dialogue, taking the time to outline your main points and supporting details ensures that your message remains focused and clear. For instance, when proposing a new project plan, presenting the objectives first, followed by the methods, expected outcomes, and potential challenges, provides a structured approach that enhances the listener's comprehension.

Feedback plays a pivotal role in refining communication skills. Engaging others in the feedback process allows one to identify areas that require improvement. Constructive feedback helps in recognizing discrepancies between what was intended to be communicated and how it was perceived. By actively seeking feedback, communicators gain insights into the effectiveness of their delivery and can make necessary adjustments. For example, after presenting a corporate strategy, soliciting feedback from colleagues can uncover whether the key messages were understood as intended or if certain aspects need clarity.

Guiding others through this iterative process of feedback and refinement is essential. Encourage open dialogue by creating an environment where individuals feel comfortable sharing their perspectives and offering critiques. This collaborative approach not only fosters mutual understanding but also cultivates a culture of continuous improvement. Remember, feedback should be specific, focusing on particular aspects of the communication rather than vague generalities.

Moreover, approaching feedback with an open mind and a willingness to adapt is crucial for personal growth in communication skills. Embracing constructive criticism without becoming defensive allows for genuine learning opportunities. It's about recognizing that effective communication is a dynamic process, requiring ongoing development and adjustment based on input from others.

Another fundamental aspect of improving communication is practicing active listening, though not covered extensively here. Active listening involves fully engaging with the speaker, making them feel heard and understood. By concentrating on what others express without planning your response prematurely, you ensure that communication flows both ways, reducing the risk of missing key points or context.

Acknowledging Non-Verbal Signals

Non-verbal communication plays a pivotal role in human interactions, often conveying messages that words alone cannot. It is an essential component of effective communication, influencing perceptions and providing depth to our interactions with others. Understanding its significance and learning how to master non-verbal cues can greatly enhance an individual's ability to communicate effectively.

Body language, as a crucial aspect of non-verbal communication, frequently communicates more than the spoken word. The way we hold ourselves, our posture, gestures, facial expressions, and eye movements all contribute to the message we are sending out. For instance, crossed arms may signal defensiveness or discomfort, while an open stance might indicate confidence and receptivity. Studies have shown that people tend to make snap judgments based on these non-verbal signals, which can greatly influence initial impressions and subsequent interactions.

Being attentive to a speaker's body language can provide a deeper context to their verbal communication. When we actively engage with both verbal and non-verbal cues during conversations, we gain a more comprehensive understanding of the message being conveyed. This attentiveness allows us to pick up on subtle nuances, such as changes in tone or shifts in posture, which might indicate hesitation, enthusiasm, or sincerity. By honing our skills in interpreting these signals, we become better equipped to respond appropriately and empathetically in various situations.

Conscious use of gestures serves as an effective tool for emphasizing key points during discussions. Gestures can underscore the importance of particular ideas, making them more memorable to the audience. For example, using hand motions to describe the size of an object or to emphasize a critical point can help clarify and reinforce the speaker's intent. Through my last thirty years, training individuals and teams in Excellence, Leadership and Communication, with a special focus in body language, I may argue that appropriate gestures can aid in expressing thoughts more clearly, helping individuals to speak in more precise, declarative sentences. When our gestures align with our verbal messages, they lend authenticity to our communication, fostering trust and understanding.

Practicing awareness of one's own non-verbal communication is critical for anyone looking to improve their interactions. Recording oneself during conversations or presentations provides valuable insights into personal non-verbal strengths and weaknesses. This practice can reveal habits or gestures that may not align with the intended message, or that inadvertently convey unintended emotions, such as nervousness or disinterest. By reviewing recordings, individuals can identify areas needing improvement and work towards aligning their body language with their verbal communication to create a more cohesive and impactful message.

Guidelines for interpreting non-verbal signals include observing the three C's: context, clusters, and congruence. Understanding the context in which a person is communicating helps in interpreting body language accurately. For instance, recognizing that someone is in a stressful environment can explain tense body language. Observing clusters means interpreting multiple signals together rather than focusing on a single gesture, ensuring a more accurate understanding of the message. Finally, assessing congruence involves checking whether the verbal message matches the non-verbal signals. Discrepancies between the two could suggest insincerity or internal conflict.

In enhancing communication through non-verbal means, implementing a few actionable steps can be beneficial. Making a conscious effort to smile can create a welcoming and approachable atmosphere, breaking down barriers and encouraging open dialogue. Regularly maintaining appropriate eye contact is another powerful tool. It demonstrates engagement and interest, fostering a connection with the other party. However, it is important to balance eye contact to avoid making the other person uncomfortable.

Using non-verbal communication to enhance messages can be particularly impactful in leadership roles. Leaders who are adept at using body language to complement their communication are often perceived as more credible and authoritative. A firm handshake, confident posture, and steady eye contact can establish immediate respect and authority in professional settings. Furthermore, these skills are invaluable when giving presentations or speaking publicly, where non-verbal elements can captivate and retain audience attention.

For those aspiring to strengthen their non-verbal communication skills, dedicating time to practice and reflection is crucial. Such effort can lead to significant improvements, transforming how one is perceived and how effectively one can communicate. These enhancements are not limited to professional contexts but extend to personal relationships as well, underscoring the universal value of mastering non-verbal communication.

Mastering non-verbal communication requires patience and deliberate practice. Each interaction presents an opportunity to refine these skills. Encouraging feedback from peers or mentors can further support growth in this area. As individuals develop a greater sensitivity to non-verbal cues, both in themselves and others, they position themselves to become more influential communicators, capable of building meaningful connections and exerting a positive influence in various aspects of life.

Final Insights

In this chapter, we explored the importance of mastering communication skills as a foundation for building influence and leadership. We delved into active listening techniques, emphasizing the value of being fully present and engaged with a speaker to foster meaningful connections. By providing reflective responses, we can affirm emotions and build trust in professional relationships. We identified common barriers to effective listening, such as distractions and biases, and highlighted the significance of overcoming these challenges through self-reflection and mindfulness. Enhancing active listening skills not only improves personal interactions but also contributes to more effective collaboration and problem-solving in professional settings.

Furthermore, crafting clear and concise messages is vital for successful communication. By avoiding jargon and structuring thoughts logically, individuals can minimize misunderstandings and resolve conflicts efficiently. Feedback plays a critical role in refining communication skills, offering opportunities for growth and improvement. Embracing constructive criticism allows communicators to adapt and enhance their delivery. Alongside verbal communication, non-verbal cues significantly impact interactions, with body language providing depth to our messages. Developing an awareness of both verbal and others' non-verbal signals enables better understanding and more authentic exchanges. Together, these communication strategies empower young professionals, mid-career individuals, and aspiring leaders to cultivate strong relationships and achieve success in their respective fields.

Chapter 7

Leadership Through Humility and Humor

When you become too big to see the small things, you are too small to see the big things. - **The Author**

Imagine yourself hosting a potluck dinner; everyone brings their best dish, and the leader ensures that the table is set with kindness and laughter, even if someone accidentally brings that weird gelatin salad nobody wants to touch!

Leading with humility and humor is a refreshing approach that challenges traditional notions of authority. To lead effectively today, leaders are encouraged to foster an environment where openness and connection thrive. By integrating humility into their interactions, leaders can create genuine connections, bridging gaps that often exist in hierarchical structures. This not only makes leaders more relatable but also cultivates trust within teams. Humor, on the other hand, serves as a valuable tool for easing tensions and creating a positive atmosphere. It isn't about being the class clown; rather, it's about strategically using humor to navigate complex situations with grace and turn potential stressors into opportunities for personal growth. A leader's ability to laugh at themselves and share light-hearted moments reinforces a shared human experience, breaking down barriers and making leadership accessible.

In this chapter, you will explore how humility enables leaders to communicate transparently, acknowledge mistakes, and seek feedback, thereby strengthening bonds with team members. The chapter delves into practical ways leaders can admit to their limitations without sacrificing respect, encouraging collaboration and the sharing of diverse ideas. Developing these qualities is essential for young professionals looking to establish themselves and mid-career individuals seeking renewal and transformation. For entrepreneurs, understanding these dynamics can mean the difference between a principled business and one fraught with miscommunication. Furthermore, the chapter highlights the importance of humor in leadership, discussing its role in transforming workplaces into cohesive communities built on mutual respect and engagement. With actionable insights, this chapter provides a roadmap for fostering organizational cultures where everyone feels valued and ready to contribute their best efforts towards achieving shared goals.

Embracing Honesty and Vulnerability

In the journey of discovering genuine leadership, one must learn the art of connecting with people on a personal level. This means integrating humility and humor into a leadership style that fosters trust and engagement, creating an environment where individuals feel both valued and motivated. As leaders venture into this path, understanding the nuances of transparent communication, acknowledging errors, soliciting feedback, and recognizing limitations are fundamental.

Transparency in leadership begins with openness about successes and failures. This approach humanizes the leader, revealing authenticity that builds trust within the team. For example, when a project meets its objectives because of collective effort, a leader who openly acknowledges this success shares more than just the victory; they share respect for the team's contributions. Conversely, during challenging times, admitting shortcomings and failures can reinforce trust rather than diminish authority. It signals to the team that their leader is honest and committed to the organization's growth over any personal agenda. Transparency not only enhances credibility but also dismantles barriers, facilitating smoother communication channels within teams.

Acknowledging mistakes is another pillar of effective and human-centric leadership. Great leaders possess the humility to admit errors without defensiveness. This acknowledgment reflects a maturity and commitment to personal as well as organizational development. Mistakes can be powerful learning tools if approached correctly. When leaders admit errors, they invite others to learn alongside them, creating a culture that values improvement over perfection. In doing so, leaders make room for innovative solutions. This practice encourages everyone in the team to own their actions and, when necessary, correct their courses without fear of retribution or shame, ultimately promoting a healthier workplace atmosphere.

Soliciting feedback embodies respect and value for team members' voices. Leaders who actively seek input demonstrate that every opinion counts and that diverse perspectives are essential to decision-making processes. Through frequent feedback sessions, leaders open dialogue pathways where ideas flow freely. Employees engaged in such environments often feel empowered and committed to the organization's goals. Over time, this inclusivity breeds a sense of ownership and belonging among team members. Feedback doesn't need to be restricted to formal meetings; informal conversations can also yield valuable insights. Not only does this foster innovation, but it also aligns the team toward shared objectives by ensuring everyone's viewpoints are considered and appreciated.

Admitting limitations is equally pivotal. No leader, regardless of experience or expertise, has all the answers. Authentically acknowledging these gaps does not signify incompetence; rather, it empowers others to step up and showcase their strengths. It encourages a culture of collaboration where team members are motivated to contribute their unique skills and knowledge towards problem-solving. This practice inherently encourages professional growth and pushes team members to assume responsibilities more confidently. When leaders recognize their constraints, it removes the traditional hierarchy's rigidity, inviting teamwork and collective problem-solving that can lead to groundbreaking outcomes.

To cultivate these traits—transparency, acknowledgement of mistakes, solicitation of feedback, and admission of limitations—leaders should follow certain guidelines. First, implement regular check-ins, both individually and within the team, to discuss challenges and successes transparently. Second, create a safe space where admitting mistakes is not met with punitive measures but is seen as opportunities for growth. Third, establish consistent feedback mechanisms where team members are encouraged to speak freely, perhaps introducing anonymous suggestions or comments to ease any hesitance. Lastly, leaders should participate in continuous self-reflection sessions to identify and understand their limitations, demonstrating a unilateral commitment to personal and professional evolution.

Using Humor to Diffuse Tension

Incorporating humor into leadership is a practical and effective way to transform the workplace atmosphere. It is not just about cracking jokes; it's an art that, when skillfully employed, diffuses tension and nurtures camaraderie. Humor is a powerful tool for leaders who seek to create environments where stress is alleviated, and teams work cohesively. By embracing light-hearted approaches, leaders can make significant strides in turning potentially stressful situations into constructive conversations. For young professionals entering the workforce or seasoned entrepreneurs wanting to build principled businesses, understanding how to utilize humor effectively can be transformative.

Light-hearted approaches are crucial for leaders aiming to navigate tense moments with grace. Imagine a scenario where a team faces a deadline, tensions rise, and productivity stalls. A leader who injects a well-timed humorous remark can ease the palpable pressure, inviting a moment of collective exhalation. This change of tone encourages team members to relax, step back from the brink of frustration, and re-engage with the task at hand more positively. The ability to view challenges through a humorous lens enables individuals to approach problems with a fresh mindset, fostering an environment ripe for innovative solutions. Guidelines suggest incorporating humor when emotions run high, reminding us that levity can transform a team's outlook and open doors to dialogue.

Creating a positive work environment is another vital outcome of humor-infused leadership. When used adeptly, humor reduces stress, which is often the nemesis of creativity and collaboration. An atmosphere thick with anxiety stifles the free exchange of ideas, while one suffused with laughter encourages out-of-the-box thinking. Teams thrive in conditions where humor is not only allowed but encouraged. Studies and my experience have shown that humor has a stress-buffering effect by helping individuals reframe their perspective on challenging situations. This reframing allows employees to see these scenarios as growth opportunities rather than threats, further solidifying relationships among colleagues. This harmony paves the way for collaboration and innovation, as individuals feel secure enough to express themselves without fear of judgment or reprisal.

Storytelling with humor is another powerful tool leaders should harness. Engaging opening lines or humorous anecdotes during meetings can captivate an audience far better than dry facts and figures. Think of a presentation where data is interwoven with a funny story relevant to the point. Not only does this keep the audience attentive, but it also makes the information stick long after the meeting ends. Humor creates memorable experiences, which are essential for retaining information and fostering teamwork. While less structured than guidelines, a light touch of humor in storytelling can transform dull meetings into dynamic exchanges, leaving lasting impressions.

Laughing together as a team unites individuals, reducing feelings of isolation and promoting inclusiveness. Laughter bridges gaps, creating connections that transcend hierarchical barriers like few other things can. It forms the glue that holds diverse teams together, enabling them to function as cohesive units even under pressure. Shared moments of humor reinforce bonds, creating a sense of belonging that inspires loyalty and commitment. This feeling of togetherness is particularly important for mid-career individuals seeking renewed motivation and those stepping into leadership roles for the first time.

When humor is woven into daily interactions, it acts as a social catalyst, enhancing communication and fostering mutual respect. Consider a workspace buzzing with laughter—a reflection of deep interpersonal trust and rapport. Humor is more than mere entertainment; it is an essential element of effective communication and relationship-building. With humor, leaders model openness and transparency, encouraging their teams to engage genuinely. Such environments are fertile ground for nurturing emerging leaders who understand that emotional intelligence and empathy are as critical as technical skills.

For young professionals, entrepreneurs, and those seeking career transformation, mastering the art of using humor in leadership can significantly enhance one's effectiveness. It equips individuals with the tools needed to inspire teams, drive engagement, and foster a thriving organizational culture. As a strategic asset, humor enriches leadership styles, making the workplace not only a place of productivity but also of joy and collaboration.

Demonstrating Respect and Appreciation

Incorporating humility and humor into leadership goes beyond just creating a pleasant atmosphere; it fundamentally reshapes how leaders interact with their teams. This approach can transform a workplace into a thriving community, where trust and engagement flourish. Effective leaders recognize that showing respect and acknowledging their team's contributions are essential to fostering this environment.

Valuing Contributions: One of the cornerstones of effective leadership is valuing each team member's contributions. When leaders try to acknowledge everyone's input, it creates an inclusive environment where all voices are heard. Such inclusivity can significantly enhance employee engagement, as individuals feel their ideas and efforts matter. To achieve this, leaders can implement several strategies. For example, during meetings, ensure that quieter team members have the opportunity to express their thoughts. Encourage open forums for idea-sharing or create digital spaces where employees can contribute ideas freely. By actively seeking contributions from all team members, leaders demonstrate that every role, regardless of its size or function, is integral to the organization's success.

Expressing Gratitude: Expressing gratitude is not just about saying "thank you," but rather about creating a culture where appreciation is woven into the fabric of daily interactions. Leaders who thank their teams regularly can enhance employee satisfaction and loyalty. Incorporating gestures like appreciation gifts, shout-outs during meetings, or organizing special events such as Employee Appreciation Week can be highly effective. Additionally, expressing gratitude should align with individual preferences— some employees may prefer public recognition, while others might appreciate a private note or a simple verbal acknowledgment. By tailoring gratitude expression to suit different personalities, leaders can strengthen individual connections and foster a sense of belonging within the team.

Celebrating Successes: Recognizing achievements, both big and small, instills pride in team accomplishments and enhances motivation among employees. Celebrations do not always need to be grand; sometimes, a simple acknowledgment of someone's hard work during a team meeting can suffice. Highlighting successes can take various forms, such as awards, certificates, or even informal gatherings to celebrate milestones. These celebrations remind team members that their efforts are not only noticed but also valued, which in turn encourages them to maintain high-performance levels. Leaders should seize the opportunity to recognize the collective achievements of the team and, when possible, highlight individual contributions, thus building a sense of camaraderie and shared purpose.

Listening Actively: Active listening is a pivotal skill for great leaders. It involves more than just hearing words; it requires understanding the message being conveyed and responding thoughtfully. Leaders who actively engage with their teams promote an atmosphere of openness and trust. This can be achieved by creating regular opportunities for feedback and dialogue, such as one-on-one check-ins, open-door policies, or anonymous surveys that allow employees to voice concerns without fear of repercussions. Through active listening, leaders demonstrate their commitment to addressing issues affecting their teams, thus reinforcing a culture of transparency and mutual respect.

Guidelines for cultivating these principles in leadership are not one-size-fits-all; they require adaptation to fit organizational contexts and individual team dynamics. However, some overarching recommendations can guide leaders in integrating these practices effectively. Firstly, lead by example. Management and team leaders should consistently model the behavior they wish to see throughout the organization. Their conduct sets a precedent for valuing contributions, expressing gratitude, celebrating successes, and listening actively.

Secondly, encourage regular feedback. Establish structured yet flexible avenues for providing positive and constructive criticism. This could include periodic performance reviews, informal check-ins, and team discussions. Emphasizing an adaptable feedback loop helps keep communication channels open and fosters continuous improvement.

Thirdly, cultivate public recognition. Utilize company meetings, emails, or internal social media platforms to celebrate achievements and milestones. Public acknowledgment not only boosts morale but also motivates others to contribute similarly.

Additionally, consider implementing peer-to-peer recognition programs. When employees recognize each other's efforts, it reinforces a supportive and collaborative team environment. Platforms, where colleagues can share kudos or acknowledgments can be instrumental in nurturing this culture.

Lastly, tailor recognition to individual preferences. Understand that personal preferences vary—while some might relish public accolades, others may appreciate a quiet thank-you or acknowledgment. By customizing how appreciation is expressed, leaders acknowledge employees' individuality and demonstrate thoughtful consideration.

Final Insights

In this chapter, we explored how integrating humility and humor into leadership can transform organizational dynamics. Leaders who embrace these traits foster an environment where trust and engagement thrive, making individuals feel valued and more motivated to contribute. By prioritizing transparent communication and admitting mistakes, leaders lay the groundwork for authenticity and mutual respect within their teams. Soliciting feedback and acknowledging limitations enable leaders to invite diverse perspectives and collaborative solutions. These practices create a workplace culture characterized by open dialogue and shared responsibility, empowering team members to perform at their best.

Moreover, using humor strategically can further enhance team cohesion and defuse tension in challenging situations. It encourages creativity and collaboration by alleviating stress and encouraging positive interactions. Leaders who skillfully incorporate humor set the tone for a supportive atmosphere where laughter breaks down hierarchical barriers and strengthens interpersonal connections. As leaders demonstrate respect and appreciation, they cultivate an inclusive environment where everyone feels acknowledged and celebrated. Such leadership fosters not just productivity but also fosters a sense of belonging and unity that drives both individual and organizational growth.

Chapter 8

Generosity as a Success Multiplier

Generosity is not just about giving; it's about sharing the joy of success with others. **- The Author**

Imagine yourself giving away slices of cake at a party; the more you share, the bigger the smiles get, and before you know it, everyone's dancing and celebrating—just don't be the one to forget the forks!

Generosity holds the possibility to act as a powerful multiplier for success, affecting both personal fulfillment and professional respect. The essence of this chapter lies in exploring how the simple act of giving can create substantial changes in various aspects of life and work. By choosing generosity, individuals not only enrich their own lives but also contribute positively to the lives of others. This approach may seem straightforward, yet it holds far-reaching consequences that extend beyond the immediate benefits. As you delve further into this exploration, you'll discover that generosity isn't merely an act of kindness; it's a strategy that can be harnessed to generate goodwill, foster strong relationships, and drive collective success.

The chapter navigates through several dimensions of generosity's impact. It examines how sharing knowledge freely can build stronger teams and organizations, enhancing collaboration and fostering an innovative culture. It highlights the significance of supporting others' aspirations, showing how mentoring and encouraging peers in their career goals can create a network of mutual growth and satisfaction. Furthermore, it discusses engaging in acts of kindness as a practical application of generosity that transforms workplace environments, making them more cohesive and supportive. By integrating these practices into daily interactions, individuals and organizations stand to gain significantly, creating a cycle of positivity and progress that benefits everyone involved. Each section of the chapter provides insights and actionable guidelines to help professionals at different stages leverage generosity as a tool for personal and organizational success, ultimately advocating for a culture where generosity is not just a virtue, but a key component of achievement.

Sharing Knowledge Freely

Sharing knowledge within an organization is a powerful tool that enhances collaboration and builds mutual respect among team members. By creating a culture where expertise is openly exchanged, individuals can foster an environment of trust and innovation. This approach not only accelerates personal and professional growth but also cultivates a sense of belonging and shared purpose.

In many organizations, the success of collaborative efforts often hinges on establishing a knowledge-sharing culture. When team members are encouraged to share their insights and skills, it paves the way for creativity and problem-solving. For example, when a marketing team shares its data analysis techniques with the product development team, they can collaboratively create products that better meet customer needs, driving innovation. Trust is built as colleagues see their input valued and utilized, making them more willing to contribute ideas in the future.

Mentorship plays a crucial role in this dynamic environment. Offering mentorship opportunities where experienced professionals guide newcomers strengthens leadership skills and fosters supportive networks. Through mentorship, leaders hone their abilities to guide and motivate others, while mentees gain valuable insights and accelerated learning paths. A junior engineer receiving guidance from a seasoned project manager not only learns technical skills but also gains insights into organizational strategies and soft skills. These interactions build a network of support that benefits both parties and the organization at large.

A pivotal aspect of cultivating this environment involves documenting and sharing lessons learned from past experiences. When teams document failures and successes alike, they preserve institutional memory that aids others in avoiding similar pitfalls and leveraging successful strategies. Consider a scenario where a software company documents a project's challenges and solutions. New teams can refer to these resources, learning from previous mistakes and becoming resilient in the face of new challenges. Such documentation acts as a reservoir of wisdom, continuously replenished by contributions across the organization.

Encouraging open dialogue further enriches this culture by promoting collective problem-solving and inclusivity. When team members feel safe to voice their thoughts and ask questions, diverse perspectives emerge, leading to more comprehensive solutions. For instance, in brainstorming sessions where all voices are heard, unique ideas that may have been overlooked come to the fore. This practice not only results in more creative outcomes but also ensures that every team member feels included and respected, elevating morale and engagement.

To effectively implement a knowledge-sharing culture, organizations should embrace certain guidelines. Leading by example is vital; senior leaders should actively engage in sharing their insights, setting a precedent for others to follow. Their visible commitment underscores the importance of openness and transparency, encouraging broader participation. Additionally, organizations need to invest in tools and platforms that facilitate seamless knowledge exchange. Platforms like intranets, document management systems, and collaboration tools enable easy access and contribution to shared knowledge pools, breaking down barriers to information flow.

Moreover, fostering cross-functional collaboration is essential in dismantling silos within an organization. Encouraging employees from various departments to interact and collaborate nurtures a holistic understanding of business objectives. Job rotations or joint projects can be effective in this regard, exposing employees to different aspects of the organization and broadening their expertise. When individuals understand how their roles contribute to the larger goals, they become more invested in the organization's success.

Recognizing and rewarding knowledge-sharing behaviors reinforces these practices. Celebrating individuals or teams that actively contribute to the organization's intellectual capital encourages others to follow suit. Such recognition can take various forms, including public acknowledgment during meetings, awards, or career advancement opportunities. This creates a positive feedback loop, embedding knowledge sharing into the organizational culture.

Embedding knowledge sharing into everyday processes ensures its sustainability. Activities such as onboarding programs, regular training sessions, and performance reviews should incorporate elements of knowledge exchange. For example, during onboarding, new hires could be paired with mentors to help them quickly acclimate and learn, setting the tone for continuous learning and knowledge sharing throughout their tenure.

Measuring the impact of these initiatives provides feedback on areas needing improvement. Establishing metrics such as the frequency of knowledge-sharing activities, employee engagement levels, and innovation rates can offer insights into the effectiveness of implemented strategies. Organizations can then refine their approaches based on this data, ensuring that the culture of sharing evolves to meet changing needs.

Implementing these guidelines enables organizations to harness the full potential of their collective intelligence. The case of a manufacturing company that adopted a comprehensive knowledge-sharing strategy exemplifies this success. By integrating cross-functional teams and a robust knowledge repository, they saw a significant increase in productivity and innovation over two years. This demonstrates the tangible benefits of investing in a knowledge-sharing culture.

Supporting Others' Aspirations

Championing the aspirations of others can act as a powerful catalyst for mutual success and enriched relationships. When individuals take proactive steps to support their peers' career goals, they not only create a culture of motivation and loyalty but also set the stage for collective achievement. Imagine an environment where colleagues actively cheer each other on, offering resources, advice, and encouragement, all with the aim of seeing one another succeed. Such an atmosphere transforms individual pursuits into shared victories, fostering bonds that are both personal and professional.

Actively nurturing the career goals of peers is not just about verbal encouragement; it extends to tangible actions that create a supportive framework. Consider, for example, the impact of mentoring programs within organizations, which pair less experienced professionals with seasoned mentors who can guide them through potential challenges and opportunities. This sort of structured support can result in higher job satisfaction and retention rates, as shown in numerous studies. By investing in each other's growth, professionals enhance their workplace culture and build a sense of camaraderie that transcends mere job titles.

Identifying and sharing opportunities with peers is another effective way to demonstrate leadership while enhancing professional respect. This involves keeping an ear to the ground for openings, whether they be job vacancies, project collaborations, or learning workshops, and being willing to share this information generously. For instance, a manager who regularly forwards details about industry conferences or skill-building webinars to their team signals that they value continued professional development. Such acts showcase leadership qualities and foster an environment of trust and openness, where knowledge and prospects are mutually exchanged. Implementing a guideline to maintain regular communication channels for sharing such opportunities can further embed this practice into the organizational culture, ensuring continuous growth and connectivity among team members.

Guidelines for providing constructive feedback can serve as a vital tool in empowering individuals to refine their skills and achieve their full potential. Constructive feedback should aim to be specific, focusing on observable actions rather than personal traits, and provide clear examples along with suggestions for improvement. Imagine a scenario where feedback becomes a staple of weekly meetings, enabling colleagues to learn from one another's experiences and mistakes without fear of judgment. Such an approach encourages transparency and builds confidence, equipping employees with the tools they need to tackle future challenges more effectively. A simple yet effective guideline would involve framing feedback within a "strengths-opportunities" model, highlighting what was done well before gently introducing areas for growth.

While celebrating the successes of others may seem intuitive, its profound impact on boosting morale and fostering appreciation cannot be overlooked. Recognizing achievements, whether big or small, instills a sense of value and belonging among team members. Consider how a monthly recognition program that highlights individual contributions not only uplifts those who are honored but also inspires their peers to strive for similar excellence. This culture of celebration contributes to a positive work environment where everyone feels appreciated and motivated to excel.

Incorporating these practices into daily interactions could lead to a remarkable transformation in workplace dynamics. Young professionals entering the workforce will find themselves in a nurturing ecosystem that values ambition and collaboration. Mid-career individuals looking for renewed motivation can regain their drive as they are supported in reaching new heights, while entrepreneurs and aspiring leaders can cultivate robust, ethically-sound businesses grounded in mutual support and respect.

Engaging in Acts of Kindness

Simple acts of kindness in the workplace can be transformative, creating an environment ripe with goodwill and strong interpersonal connections. These small gestures, often overlooked, hold the power to nurture relationships and enhance morale, benefiting both individuals and the organization at large.

Consider the impact of a note left anonymously on a colleague's desk, praising their dedication or congratulating them for completing a challenging project. Such expressions of appreciation, though brief, can significantly boost morale and encourage a sense of belonging. Acts like these demonstrate how small efforts can foster substantial positive changes in the workplace atmosphere. When employees feel valued, they are more likely to contribute positively, fostering a culture where kindness becomes commonplace. This openness inevitably enhances collaboration and drives collective team success (Boosting Workplace Morale: Simple Random Acts of Kindness Ideas for Work, 2024).

Volunteering together as a team is another powerful way to strengthen bonds while contributing to a greater cause. Engaging in community service projects cultivates solidarity, reflecting a committed stance towards social responsibility. Organizations that incorporate volunteering into their activities not only enhance their communities but also create memorable experiences for their teams. These shared experiences often lead to deeper understanding and respect among colleagues, translating into a more cohesive unit ready to tackle challenges collaboratively. For instance, organizing a day at a local charity event allows team members to work side-by-side outside the usual office setting, helping break down barriers and establish open communication.

Creating initiatives such as kindness challenges can be instrumental in sustaining motivation and engagement over time. These challenges can take many forms, from encouraging employees to perform random acts of kindness daily to organizing monthly events promoting positivity throughout the workplace. For example, initiating a 'pay it forward' week, where each employee is encouraged to perform a kind act for another person without expecting anything in return, can motivate employees to think creatively about how they can positively impact others. The ripple effect from such actions often leads to increased camaraderie and engagement.

Recognizing acts of kindness, although not requiring specific guidelines, can serve as an important reinforcement of its value within the workplace. Publicly acknowledging colleagues who have gone out of their way to assist others can inspire greater participation across all levels of the organization. This recognition doesn't have to be formal; even a mention during a team meeting or a shout-out in a company newsletter can validate and encourage the behavior. When employees see that acts of kindness are appreciated and celebrated, they are more likely to continue these behaviors, creating a cycle of positivity and cooperation. Leaders play a crucial role here by setting the tone and demonstrating through their actions that kindness is integral to the organization's success.

Practicing small daily acts of kindness can be guided in simple ways. Managers might suggest employees start their day by writing a quick thank-you email or offering help to a colleague facing tight deadlines. Even everyday courtesies like holding the door open or sharing words of encouragement in stressful times can make a significant difference. Developing these habits doesn't require grand gestures but relies on consistency and sincerity.

When organizations prioritize kindness, the benefits multiply rapidly. A study highlighted in a prominent research article explains how kindness can improve workplace culture and productivity. It was found that leaders who embrace kindness create a cooperative culture, enhancing both employee satisfaction and efficiency (Sezer et al., 2021). The inclusive atmosphere that results from widespread acts of kindness has been shown to reduce stress and turnover rates, ultimately driving better performance and job satisfaction. Moreover, when employees witness acts of kindness becoming the norm, they're inspired to pay it forward, perpetuating a cycle of generosity and support throughout the organization.

Bringing It All Together

Through exploring generosity in knowledge-sharing, supporting others' aspirations, and engaging in acts of kindness, this chapter has unfolded the layers of how these practices enrich workplace dynamics. Sharing expertise opens doors to collaboration, fostering an atmosphere where trust and mutual respect flourish. Encouraging mentorship and capturing organizational memory through shared lessons further solidifies personal and professional bonds. By aligning roles with a broader vision, individuals find purpose and accountability within their contributions, ultimately driving collective success.

Supporting peers' career goals transforms individual pursuits into shared victories. Structured mentorships and leadership demonstrated through sharing opportunities contribute to a cycle of empowerment and cooperation, enhancing professional respect. Simultaneously, acts of kindness strengthen interpersonal connections, nurturing a culture of positivity and inclusivity. The benefits of these practices resonate throughout organizations, promoting satisfaction and motivation while reducing stress. As young professionals, mid-career individuals, and aspiring leaders integrate these principles, they pave the way toward building ethical and supportive work environments where everyone thrives.

Chapter 9

Nurturing Creativity and Innovation

Creativity is intelligence; having fun is seeing what others see and thinking what no one else has ever thought. The impossible is just something that no one has done... yet! **- The Author**

Imagine yourself gardening; you plant the seeds of ideas, water them with encouragement, and sometimes, you even have to laugh when a wild weed pops up—because every garden needs a little chaos to remind us that nature thrives in unpredictability!

Nurturing creativity and innovation are an essential component of both personal and professional growth. It involves creating conditions that empower individuals to think outside the box and explore uncharted territories, leading to groundbreaking solutions. Embracing creativity not only enriches individual experiences but also brings tangible benefits to organizations and communities, sparking new ideas and driving progress. While many recognize the value of innovation, fostering the right environment for it can be challenging, often requiring a deliberate effort to cultivate spaces and mindsets that support creative exploration.

In this chapter, we delve into various strategies and principles that are foundational to nurturing creativity and innovation. We will explore how physical environments, like workspaces designed with attention to light, color, and comfort, can positively impact our creative capabilities. The discussion will extend to psychological factors, emphasizing the importance of safety and openness in encouraging inventive ideas without fear of criticism. Furthermore, the chapter will highlight the role of autonomy in task execution, showcasing how individual freedom fuels creativity by allowing unique approaches to problem-solving. We'll also examine how diverse resources and interdisciplinary collaboration enrich perspectives and inspire novel thinking. By examining these elements, the chapter aims to provide readers with practical insights into designing environments and practices that foster continuous innovation and creative growth.

Creating an Environment Conducive to Creativity

Creating an environment conducive to creativity can significantly enhance the potential for innovation. The physical space in which we work plays a profound role in shaping our mindset and productivity. Consider how the inclusion of inspiring colors, sufficient natural light, and overall comfort can transform a mundane setting into one brimming with possibilities. Research has shown that exposure to different hues influences mood and thought processes. Warm tones might energize, whereas cool colors can induce calmness, both crucial at various stages of the creative process.

Lighting is another pivotal factor. Natural light boosts mood and concentration, fostering a positive mental state crucial for innovative thinking. In contrast, poorly lit environments may contribute to fatigue and hinder our ability to process information effectively. Adding elements of comfort, such as ergonomic furniture and personalized decor, can make individuals feel at ease and more open to exploring new ideas. Workspaces designed with these elements allow mental barriers to dissolve, ushering in a fresh wave of creativity.

Psychological safety in an organization is equally vital for nurturing an innovative spirit. When team members feel secure in sharing unconventional or risky ideas without fear of ridicule, it encourages them to venture beyond their comfort zones. This trust-building approach creates an atmosphere where dialogue thrives, and new concepts emerge organically. By establishing a culture that values every input, leaders can motivate employees to partake in collaborative brainstorming sessions, ultimately leading to breakthrough solutions.

To instill psychological safety, organizations must actively promote open communication and respect diverse perspectives. Encouraging constructive feedback rather than punitive measures when ideas fail ensure that individuals remain motivated to innovate. As noted in my trainings on creativity with in my courses and International Referral Marketing companies, a supportive environment often ties back to management practices and organizational climate. Hence, fostering psychological safety is not just about mitigating risks but empowering teams to think boldly.

The provision of autonomy in task approaches further complements the drive toward creativity. When individuals have the freedom to determine how they wish to tackle a problem, they are more likely to experiment and derive original solutions. Traditional top-down structures may impose restrictions that constrain creative thought. However, by offering flexibility, organizations enable employees to harness their skills and passions effectively.

For instance, companies like Google have famously adopted the "20% time" policy, allowing employees to dedicate a portion of their work hours to projects of personal interest. This policy has led to the development of numerous successful products, demonstrating how autonomy can foster innovation. Autonomy also cultivates ownership and responsibility, encouraging proactive engagement with challenges.

Finally, incorporating diverse resources, including elements from nature and various creative tools, provides stimuli that inspires and broadens thinking. Exposure to nature, even through simple actions like taking walks or viewing greenery, has been linked to improved cognitive function and creativity. Nature acts as a calming presence that refreshes the mind, making it more receptive to new ideas.

Furthermore, access to an array of creative tools, from digital applications to traditional art supplies, can assist in breaking out of conventional thinking patterns. These resources enable individuals to express themselves in unique ways, facilitating the exploration of unconventional solutions. Offering opportunities to engage with different mediums—be it writing, sketching, or prototyping—

enhances creative capacity by catering to diverse thinking styles and preferences.

Organizations can also benefit from varied inputs by drawing from interdisciplinary collaborations. Engaging professionals from different fields can introduce novel perspectives, enriching the collective pool of ideas. This diversity cultivates an inclusive culture where creativity flourishes naturally.

Encouraging Brainstorming and Experimentation

Active participation in brainstorming sessions and experimentation is crucial for sparking creativity and fostering innovation. Brainstorming, by design, is an inclusive process that thrives on the diverse perspectives and energies of a group. Utilizing structured techniques like mind mapping can transform this potential into tangible outputs.

Mind mapping is a visual tool that encourages participants to expand their thoughts organically, connecting ideas and elements in a way that linear thinking might overlook. Imagine a team gathered around a digital whiteboard, each member contributing ideas non-verbally through connected nodes. This method ensures that even quieter members have their thoughts captured and recognized. Notably, it maximizes participation by creating an environment where every contribution builds upon others, forming a network of ideas rather than a single thread. The collective energy and diversity of input enrich the end result, pushing beyond initial boundaries and inviting new intersections of thought.

Rapid prototyping serves as another pillar in the creative process, enabling ideas generated during brainstorming to be swiftly brought into the physical or digital realm. It allows teams to test concepts quickly and gather feedback efficiently. For instance, a new product idea might go through several iterations in just hours or days, with tangible versions or mockups created to visualize concepts. These prototypes can then be tested, critiqued, and refined repeatedly. Feedback becomes an integral part of the process, fueling continuous cycles of creativity and improvement. The iterative nature allows for adjustments based on real-world critiques, keeping the momentum of innovation alive and thriving.

While engaging in these practices, promoting divergent thinking remains essential. Divergent thinking stands as a counterbalance to traditional problem-solving approaches. By encouraging the exploration of varied ideas and embracing open-ended questions, it widens the spectrum of possibilities. When participants feel free to question assumptions and propose outlandish ideas, they break away from conventional constraints. For example, considering the potential applications of a technology beyond its intended use can lead to groundbreaking innovations. Encouraging such broadmindedness broadens perspectives, enabling teams to see beyond immediate limitations and discover novel solutions.

Incorporating playful methods into brainstorming sessions can further enhance creativity. Introducing elements of gamification, where tasks are designed to include game-like features such as scoring points or achieving levels, transforms the process into something enjoyable. This fun approach not only relieves the pressure often associated with ideation but also breaks down habitual thought patterns. Picture a brainstorming session where ideas are pitched in a role-playing scenario or where rewards are given for the most unconventional suggestions. These playful tactics make experimentation less intimidating and help reduce stress, opening up pathways to more relaxed, imaginative thinking.

The integration of technology bolsters these strategies, extending the capabilities of traditional brainstorming. Tools such as collaborative whiteboards enable real-time visualization of ideas, allowing instant feedback and iteration. Online idea management systems streamline the collection and organization of numerous suggestions, enhancing the efficiency of managing large volumes of input. Moreover, video conferencing enhancements facilitate interactive sessions by using screen-sharing features, breakout rooms, and real-time collaboration. By transcending physical limitations, technology adds a dynamic dimension to the process, encouraging engagement and broadening participation scope.

Overcoming creative blocks remains an ongoing challenge within brainstorming and experimentation. Creative blocks, often characterized by mental stagnation, can halt the flow of ideas. Implementing strategies to overcome these barriers is vital for maintaining the vibrancy and productivity of the sessions. Techniques such as mindfulness exercises can introduce a state of calm, focusing the mind and reducing stress. Changing the physical environment by conducting sessions outdoors or in varied settings can provide fresh stimuli, triggering new ideas. Drawing inspiration from external sources, whether it's art, literature, or nature, injects diverse influences that can revitalize creativity.

Encouraging participation from all attendees is pivotal for successful brainstorming sessions. Structured facilitation ensures that everyone has an opportunity to contribute, with designated facilitators guiding discussions and using techniques like round-robin brainstorming. This systematic approach ensures no voice goes unheard, capturing the full range of insights and experiences available. Emphasizing the value of diverse input enriches the brainstorming session, drawing from unique personal experiences and fostering inclusivity. Neurodiversity should also be recognized as a valuable component, appreciating the different cognitive abilities that lead to innovative and unconventional ideas.

Lastly, incorporating feedback into the brainstorming process is critical for refining and enhancing the ideas generated. Constructive criticism allows participants to focus on improvement, and iterative refinement uses feedback loops to build upon initial concepts. Anonymous feedback mechanisms can empower individuals to share honest opinions without fear, while seeking input from diverse sources within and outside the team brings valuable insights. Scheduling dedicated sessions to discuss and integrate feedback ensures the team collectively evaluates and incorporates useful input, elevating the quality of ideas through collaboration and shared wisdom.

Seeking Diverse Perspectives

In a world constantly reshaping its boundaries through collaboration and creativity, the infusion of diverse viewpoints serves as a catalyst for innovation. The idea that cross-disciplinary collaboration encourages fresh and innovative solutions takes center stage in this realm. By integrating unique insights from varied fields, individuals can challenge assumptions and rethink conventions, thereby nurturing groundbreaking ideas that might otherwise remain dormant.

Let's consider the concept of cross-disciplinary collaboration, which is akin to assembling a tapestry woven from threads of different specialties and expertise. For instance, when a software development team includes professionals from psychology or sociology, it enriches the creative process by shedding light on user behavior and societal trends that might not be immediately apparent to tech specialists alone. This integration allows for designing products or services that resonate deeply with diverse audiences, thus driving innovation.

Similarly, embracing inclusive hiring practices is paramount to cultivating environments rich in creativity and problem-solving capabilities. By deliberately building teams with varied backgrounds, experiences, and perspectives, organizations can harness a broader spectrum of ideas and approaches. Diverse teams are more equipped to tackle complex problems, as they bring together a multitude of viewpoints that foster comprehensive discussions and novel solutions. An effective way to implement this is by ensuring recruitment processes not only target different demographics but also embrace various skillsets, making room for professionals who may not fit traditional molds but offer invaluable insights.

Feedback loops stand out as another vital component in refining ideas. These loops facilitate the transformation of potential blind spots into opportunities for growth through regular engagement with stakeholders. When feedback is solicited from a broad range of voices—be it customers, partners, or even competitors—it provides a more holistic view, enabling creators to see beyond their immediate perceptions and adjust their strategies accordingly. For example, tech companies often run beta tests where users provide input on functionality and user experience, allowing the developers to refine their products before general release. This iterative process not only improves product quality but also enhances customer satisfaction by actively involving them in the creation journey.

Moreover, cultural exchange plays an essential role in enriching the brainstorming sessions with global perspectives. Breaking down cultural barriers opens new avenues for creativity by challenging norms and introducing alternative ways of thinking. In a business setting, bringing together international teams can lead to more inventive solutions by merging different cultural contexts and values. This diversity forces teams to confront and reconcile differences, ultimately leading to more robust and well-rounded outcomes. For instance, multinational corporations like Unilever have seen success by leveraging multicultural teams to tailor products to diverse markets, ensuring relevance and resonance across geographical boundaries.

Inclusive hiring practices call for particular attention as they directly contribute to building an enriched creativity pool within an organization. By recruiting talent from diverse backgrounds, companies ensure a mix of experiences and perspectives, enhancing both creativity and problem-solving. Creating guidelines for inclusive hiring can help establish a framework for organizations to follow. This might include practices such as training recruiters to recognize unconscious biases and establishing policies that prioritize diversity metrics. Encouraging mentorship programs where seasoned leaders guide newcomers from varied backgrounds can also foster an environment of mutual learning and encouragement.

Final Insights

This chapter has delved into the essential elements that foster creativity and drive innovation in both personal and professional contexts. By creating environments tailored to support imaginative thinking, individuals and teams can unlock new levels of productivity and problem-solving potential. From optimizing physical spaces with appropriate colors and lighting to ensuring psychological safety within organizations, each aspect contributes to an atmosphere where creative ideas can flourish. Encouraging autonomy and integrating diverse resources and perspectives further enriches this setting, allowing everyone to bring their unique strengths to the table, ultimately leading to groundbreaking solutions.

Additionally, active engagement through brainstorming and experimentation anchors the innovative process. Techniques like mind mapping and rapid prototyping invite varied contributions and refine ideas efficiently. Emphasizing diversity ensures a broad spectrum of input, enriching the creative outcomes that stem from these sessions. Leveraging technology enhances these efforts, making collaboration more dynamic and inclusive. As readers explore ways to cultivate creativity in their environments, embracing these strategies will empower them to push boundaries, challenge conventions, and nurture growth across all facets of their lives and careers.

Chapter 10

Building Resilience in the Face of Adversity

Resilience is not about never falling; it's about rising every time we fall, knowing that life doesn't get easier or more forgiving, but we grow stronger and more resilient with each challenge. - **The Author**

Imagine yourself trying to teach a cat to fetch; it might seem frustrating at first, but with patience and a few treats, you might just end up with a feline that takes on challenges with grace and a good dose of sass!

Building resilience in the face of adversity is a vital skill that equips individuals to thrive amidst life's inevitable challenges. This chapter delves into the intricate nature of setbacks and highlights their indispensable role in personal and professional development. Rather than viewing obstacles as insurmountable barriers, understanding them as opportunities for growth can transform one's outlook on adversity. By fostering resilience, individuals are better prepared to navigate difficulties with grace and emerge stronger from each encounter.

Throughout this chapter, you will explore various dimensions of resilience, including emotional resilience and the importance of acknowledging our natural responses to setbacks. It emphasizes the value of self-reflection and the adoption of a growth mindset, which together form a foundation for overcoming adversity. The chapter also underscores the significance of establishing supportive networks and environments where open communication thrives. Through real-world examples and insights, you will gain practical strategies to build resilience, thus empowering them to handle life's ups and downs with wisdom and confidence.

Understanding the Nature of Setbacks

Resilience in the face of adversity is a vital skill that enables individuals to thrive, especially when encountering setbacks. A setback, by definition, is a disruption that stalls progress, yet it is an unavoidable aspect of both personal and professional growth. Understanding its role as an essential component of development can transform our perspective and lead to positive outcomes. Setbacks provide unique, often hidden opportunities for reflection, learning, and ultimately, advancement.

When we encounter a setback, it's easy to feel disheartened or view it as a failure. However, reframing these experiences as opportunities allows us to delve into self-reflection and gain insights that might have remained overlooked. Consider Thomas Edison's experience of inventing the lightbulb; he famously stated, "I have not failed. I've just found 10,000 ways that won't work." This mindset exemplifies how setbacks serve as steppingstones to innovation and success. Dwelling on what went wrong lacks productivity, whereas extracting lessons from the experience can drive future improvements.

Sharing experiences of setbacks fosters a sense of community and collective growth. When individuals openly discuss their struggles, they contribute to a culture where challenges are normalized and seen as integral to the journey toward success. In professional settings, peer storytelling of setbacks encourages empathy and understanding among colleagues, aiding the development of stronger support networks. As more people share their stories, the stigma around setbacks diminishes, paving the way for a more open exchange of ideas and experiences.

Acknowledging the emotional responses elicited by setbacks is crucial for managing them effectively. Emotions such as frustration, disappointment, or anxiety are natural reactions that need validation. Ignoring these emotions can lead to exacerbated stress or reduced productivity. Instead, recognizing and addressing these feelings promotes healthier coping mechanisms. For instance, Jane, a young professional, faced rejection in her first job application. By acknowledging her disappointment, she was able to reflect on her approach, seek constructive feedback, and eventually secure a position that matched her aspirations.

Emotional resilience is a key factor in navigating setbacks with grace and composure. It involves adapting to change and bouncing back stronger from adversity. Individuals can build emotional resilience by practicing self-reflection, which helps in understanding emotional triggers and patterns. This insight arms them with strategies to handle similar challenges in the future. Developing a support network also plays a significant role, allowing individuals to lean on others for guidance and encouragement during tough times.

One effective approach to fostering emotional resilience is cultivating a growth mindset—a belief that abilities and intelligence can develop through dedication and hard work. This perspective encourages viewing setbacks not as dead ends, but as valuable learning experiences. For entrepreneurs, this mindset is particularly beneficial as the path of building a business is fraught with uncertainties and obstacles. Recognizing each hurdle as an opportunity for adaptation and refinement fuels both personal and organizational growth.

To further support resilience, it's important to create environments where people feel safe expressing their thoughts and emotions. Open communication nurtures trust and transparency, leading to more effective problem-solving. Celebrating successes, even small ones, builds confidence and motivation, reinforcing the idea that progress, despite setbacks, is achievable. Moreover, integrating regular practices like mindfulness or deep breathing can help manage stress, enabling clearer thinking during challenging situations.

Setbacks, while sometimes difficult to endure, forge the path to improvement if viewed through the right lens. Each challenge offers the potential to learn more about oneself and the world, contributing to an ongoing cycle of personal growth. By embracing setbacks as necessary components of the journey, individuals can navigate life's inevitable ups and downs with increased fortitude and wisdom.

Cultivating a Support Network

In the journey of life and career, having a reliable support system is not just beneficial; it is essential. A robust network of supportive individuals can significantly impact one's ability to navigate challenges and maintain resilience in the face of adversity. Young professionals, mid-career individuals, and entrepreneurs alike can benefit greatly from cultivating connections that offer both emotional and practical assistance.

A strong support network typically includes friends, family, colleagues, and mentors who each play a distinct role in providing the necessary backing during tough times. For young professionals entering the workforce, tapping into a network of experienced mentors can be invaluable. Mentors provide guidance based on their experiences, help in career decision-making, and often act as sounding boards for novel ideas. Similarly, family members can offer unwavering emotional support, creating a safe environment where one can share concerns without judgment.

Friends also contribute significantly by being there during celebratory moments and offering solace during low periods. Colleagues can provide insight into workplace dynamics and collaborate on projects that foster professional growth. Knowing that someone is in your corner enhances confidence, encouraging individuals to tackle challenges head-on rather than retreating when obstacles arise.

Building trust within this network is fundamental to ensuring that relationships endure through thick and thin. Trust does not develop overnight but instead builds overtime through open and honest communication. Being transparent about one's needs, expectations, and boundaries allows for reciprocal understanding and respect. Regularly sharing thoughts and feelings with those in your support network helps ensure everyone remains aligned in their mutual objectives. This consistent reinforcement of shared values strengthens the relational bond, making it easier to rely on these individuals when adversity strikes.

Open communication forms the bedrock of any supportive relationship, ensuring that misunderstandings are minimized, and issues can be addressed promptly. For instance, sharing both achievements and struggles with your support group not only reinforces the bonds but also opens up possibilities for constructive feedback and encouragement. This dynamic ensures that support systems do not stagnate but evolve alongside individual growth and challenges.

Beyond personal connections, professional support such as therapy or coaching offers specialized strategies for managing stress and developing resilience. Engaging with a therapist or coach provides access to tailored approaches and coping mechanisms that might not be available through informal networks alone. These professionals offer an objective perspective, helping individuals identify patterns or behaviors that may hinder progress. Their expertise becomes particularly significant when one faces prolonged stress or requires assistance in making critical life decisions. The structured guidance from therapy or coaching sessions ensures that one can approach challenges with a clear mind and fortified resolve.

Furthermore, regular engagement with your support network is crucial for maintaining and strengthening these vital relationships. Sometimes, people fall into the trap of reaching out only during crises, which can inadvertently strain the connection. Instead, consistent interactions — whether through casual meetups, virtual conversations, or collaborative projects — help sustain these ties. Setting aside time to connect with friends, family, and mentors demonstrates commitment and appreciation, reinforcing the mutual importance of these relationships.

Such ongoing dedication to nurturing one's support system ensures that the network will stand firm against future adversities. When the inevitable challenges of life or work arise, individuals who have invested in their support systems find themselves better equipped to handle stress and mitigate its impact on their well-being.

The significance of a strong support network extends beyond immediate interpersonal benefits; it also influences physical and mental health. According to my experience in my Courses about Excellence, Communication and Leadership, social support networks can lower levels of stress, enhance emotional well-being, and boost self-esteem. They can serve as buffers against anxiety and depression, aiding in recovery and promoting overall life satisfaction. Thus, investing in these relationships has far-reaching positive effects, underscoring why they should be prioritized throughout one's personal and professional journey.

For entrepreneurs and aspiring leaders, building a principled business involves leveraging a similarly robust support system. Business mentors can offer insights into ethical practices, while peers in similar fields can provide accountability and inspiration. The shared experiences within entrepreneurial support groups can act as catalysts for innovation, highlighting opportunities and risks others might not see. Engaging with a diverse array of voices enriches one's perspective, ensuring that leadership decisions reflect a balanced and informed viewpoint.

Practicing Stress Management Techniques

Navigating adversity is an inevitable part of life. However, by adopting practical techniques to manage stress, we can bolster our resilience and emerge stronger. One highly effective method for managing stress involves incorporating breathing and mindfulness exercises into daily routines. These practices have been shown to reduce acute stress responses significantly. When faced with a stressful situation, the body triggers a "fight or flight" response, which can be overwhelming and distracting. By engaging in mindful breathing, individuals can activate their parasympathetic nervous system, promoting a sense of calm and focus. Techniques such as deep breathing or guided meditation can serve as immediate tools to counteract stress and regain clarity, allowing individuals to address challenges more effectively.

Additionally, physical activity plays a crucial role in managing stress and enhancing resilience. Exercise induces the release of endorphins, often referred to as the brain's natural painkillers and mood elevators. Regular physical activity, whether it's a brisk walk, yoga, or a workout session, doesn't just improve physical health but also offers profound mental health benefits. Engaging in exercise provides a necessary break from stressors, allowing individuals to reset and approach problems with renewed vigor and perspective. Moreover, consistent physical activity leads to better sleep patterns, which are essential for processing emotions and thoughts effectively.

Another avenue to explore for stress mitigation is the use of creative outlets. Activities like drawing, writing, or playing an instrument provide excellent means for emotional expression and release. Creative pursuits can act as a distraction from the pressures of daily life, enabling the mind to take a temporary respite from stress. Furthermore, engaging in creative tasks encourages problem-solving skills. When individuals immerse themselves in a creative process, they often discover unexpected solutions or new approaches to existing challenges. This ability to think outside the box is invaluable when facing adversity, as it fosters a mindset that is open to transformation and growth.

Establishing stable routines filled with self-care practices is another critical step toward building resilience. In times of uncertainty, having a predictable structure helps mitigate anxiety and create a sense of control. Incorporating self-care activities, such as regular sleep schedules, nutritious meals, and relaxation rituals, ensures that the body and mind receive the nourishment they need to function optimally. When these practices become routine, they form an anchor that individuals can rely on amidst chaos, providing stability and reassurance that fosters a resilient mindset.

Creating guidelines for these practices can further enhance their effectiveness. Recognizing typical human responses like denial or fear and stimulating proactive behaviors can greatly aid in navigating stress. Reframing setbacks as learning opportunities rather than penalties encourages a growth-oriented outlook. For instance, approaching a setback with the mindset that it is merely a hurdle to overcome rather than an insurmountable obstacle allows individuals to maintain momentum even in difficult times. Integrating positive reinforcement strategies can serve as motivators, celebrating small victories and progress along the way.

Concluding Thoughts

In this chapter, we explored how resilience is pivotal for individuals striving to excel amidst challenges. By understanding setbacks as natural components of growth, not barriers, we can transform adversity into steppingstones toward success. Setbacks offer unique opportunities for introspection and learning, allowing us to become more adept and innovative in our personal and professional lives. The examples discussed emphasize that by reframing these experiences, we build emotional resilience, which in turn fosters strength and adaptability through continuous self-reflection and support networks.

Moreover, the cultivation of a supportive network is essential for enduring life's ups and downs. Whether in the early stages of a career or navigating mid-career shifts, having reliable connections provides both emotional solace and practical advice. This network is strengthened by open communication and shared experiences, creating a culture where challenges are seen as integral to the journey rather than exceptions. As we embrace setbacks with this resilient mindset and leverage the guidance from our circles, we equip ourselves with the tools necessary to thrive in any scenario.

Chapter 11

Mastering the Art of Persuasion

Mastering the greatest ability in business means understanding and connecting with others, reminding us that persuasion often holds more power than force in influencing their actions. **- The Author**

Imagine yourself trying to convince a toddler to eat vegetables; you might need to put on a little puppet show, sprinkle in some creativity, and offer a side of dessert as a sweet deal—with a pinch of laughter to keep the mood light!

Mastering the art of persuasion is an invaluable skill in navigating both personal and professional landscapes. It encompasses understanding how to effectively communicate ideas, inspire action, and influence outcomes through a strategic blend of logic and emotional engagement. By honing persuasive abilities, individuals can transform ordinary interactions into powerful exchanges that lead to meaningful change. In today's competitive world, whether one is stepping into a new career, seeking to revitalize their current path, or aiming to create a successful business, mastering persuasion offers considerable advantages. The ability to articulate ideas clearly and connect with others on a deeper level enhances leadership potential and opens doors to numerous opportunities. As you embark on this exploration of persuasion, consider how refining these skills can impact your journey, allowing you to build stronger relationships and achieve lasting success.

In this chapter, we delve into the core principles of effective persuasion, focusing on behaviors and techniques that can significantly enhance influence. We explore key concepts such as reciprocity and consistency—factors that drive human interaction and response. These foundational elements reveal why small gestures and commitments can have significant impacts on cooperation and motivation within teams and organizations. We'll examine how businesses leverage these principles to foster customer loyalty and employee dedication. Additionally, we'll provide insights into practical applications across various contexts, from entrepreneurship to mid-career development. Through understanding how to balance emotional intelligence with ethical practices, you'll gain tools to empower yourself and others, fostering a positive and productive environment. As you engage with these ideas, you'll uncover ways to enhance your persuasive skills and apply them effectively in different facets of your life and work.

Understanding Reciprocity and Consistency Principles

In the journey of mastering persuasion, understanding foundational behavioral principles can dramatically enhance our capacity to influence others positively. Central to this are the concepts of reciprocity and consistency—two powerful levers that drive human interactions and responses.

Reciprocity is one of the cornerstones of effective persuasion. The principle is simple: when you give something of value to others, they feel a natural obligation to return the favor. This is deeply embedded in human psychology and social norms. For instance, consider a scenario at work where a colleague offers assistance on a challenging project without being asked. This unprovoked act often encourages recipients to reciprocate in kind, perhaps by offering support on future assignments or sharing valuable insights. In the workplace, such actions don't just strengthen professional bonds but also cultivate an environment of mutual respect and cooperation.

A compelling aspect of reciprocity is its effectiveness, even with small gestures. A seemingly insignificant act, like bringing a coworker their favorite coffee, can set off a chain reaction of goodwill. These minor acts accumulate over time, fostering a culture where team members routinely go out of their way to assist each other. Such interactions reinforce a sense of shared purpose and generosity, which are critical for cohesive teamwork.

Consistency, another vital persuasive tool, taps into the human desire to be congruent with previous actions or beliefs. Once people commit to something small, they are more likely to follow through with larger commitments related to that initial promise. This is evident in how businesses use introductory offers to secure customer loyalty. By convincing someone to take an initial step, like signing up for a free trial, companies create a commitment. Customers who engage with the brand this way often define themselves as users and are consequently more inclined to make future purchases, aligning with their newly established identity.

The power of consistency is also prevalent in personal development within the workforce. Employees who publicly commit to certain goals or standards are likelier to stick to them due to a self-imposed sense of accountability. For example, when an individual expresses a desire to improve their public speaking skills by committing to a weekly practice group, they begin to see themselves as someone dedicated to personal growth. This self-perception fuels ongoing efforts and dedication.

When reciprocity and consistency are combined thoughtfully, their persuasive impact is amplified. Consider a manager looking to motivate their team. By initially showing appreciation through a small token of gratitude—perhaps a handwritten note acknowledging hard work—they activate reciprocity. Team members feel valued and are thus more inclined to reciprocate with increased engagement or performance. If the manager consistently recognizes and celebrates achievements, it reinforces employees' commitment to maintaining high standards, creating a cycle of positivity and dedication.

Implementing these strategies requires mindful execution. Start by identifying opportunities to offer genuine and personalized gestures that resonate with your audience. Ensure these actions are both unexpected and relevant, maximizing their reciprocal potential. Coupled with the tactic of nurturing small, consistent commitments, you pave the way for larger, enduring changes.

For entrepreneurs and aspiring leaders, these principles hold particular importance. Building a principled business involves not just transactional exchanges but fostering deep-rooted trust and commitment among stakeholders. By practicing reciprocity, entrepreneurs can build meaningful relationships with customers and partners. Providing value upfront—such as offering expert advice or free resources—can engender loyalty and elevate brand perception, yielding long-term benefits.

Similarly, using consistency in messaging and operations helps solidify a business's reputation. When companies consistently deliver on promises and prioritize customer satisfaction, they establish reliability that attracts and retains clients. Employees, too, are more motivated if they see management living up to stated values and leading by example.

Communicating Benefits Over Features

Focusing on benefits in persuasive communication is essential for connecting with your audience and inspiring action. Understanding what truly resonates with people allows you to craft messages that not only capture attention but also drive engagement and decision-making.

Begin with a deep understanding of your audience's values. Knowing their interests, beliefs, and motivations enables you to tailor your message to align closely with what matters most to them. When communicating persuasively, it's crucial to emphasize the benefits that directly relate to these core values. Whether you're addressing young professionals keen on career growth or entrepreneurs looking for ethical business practices, your approach should be nuanced and considerate of their specific needs and aspirations. This understanding promotes an impactful dialogue where the audience feels heard and valued.

A significant aspect of persuasive messaging lies in transforming technical features into relatable benefits. Often, messages are laden with jargon and complex details that can alienate rather than attract. Simplifying these features by highlighting their practical applications makes them more accessible. For instance, when introducing a new software tool, instead of dwelling on technical specifications, illustrate how it saves time or boosts productivity—benefits that resonate universally. Presenting tangible outcomes over abstract traits helps bridge the gap between what is offered and what is needed, making persuasion more effective.

Storytelling emerges as a vital tool in emphasizing benefits. Human beings naturally gravitate towards stories, finding comfort and connection in narratives. By weaving anecdotes, case studies, or hypothetical scenarios into your communication, you bring benefits to life. Storytelling presents opportunities to creatively embed benefits within a narrative framework, making them not just seen but felt. Imagine sharing a success story of a young professional who used a particular leadership technique to achieve remarkable results; this illustrates the benefit in a compelling way, encouraging others to envision similar successes.

Highlighting benefits is not just about immediate impact; it's about ensuring long-term message retention and fostering a meaningful connection. When an audience perceives clear advantages, they're likely to remember your message and reflect on it over time. This enduring resonance can inspire change and commitment beyond the initial interaction. Consider a presentation advocating environmentally friendly practices by focusing on the long-term benefits, such as cost savings and sustainability, the message becomes memorable, prompting ongoing reflection and potential lifestyle changes.

For young professionals entering the workforce, understanding how focusing on benefits can enhance their persuasive efforts is critical. In competitive environments, being able to articulate how one's contributions offer tangible value can set individuals apart. By continually aligning their proposals and ideas with the desires and goals of employers, they increase their chances of recognition and advancement.

Mid-career individuals facing stagnation can harness the power of benefits-focused communication to rekindle motivation and promote personal growth. By presenting ideas that align with organizational goals while highlighting how these initiatives benefit both the company and themselves, they create pathways for renewed enthusiasm and forward movement. Such strategic emphasis on mutual benefit can re-energize careers and pave the way for increased influence and opportunity.

Entrepreneurs and aspiring leaders benefit enormously from mastering benefits-focused persuasion. Building strong, principled businesses requires clarity in communication and genuine engagement with stakeholders. By consistently showcasing how their products or services positively impact customers' lives, they not only cultivate consumer trust but also build a solid foundation for lasting business relationships. Ethical persuasion through authentic benefit demonstration fosters a positive workplace culture where team members feel inspired and committed to collective success.

Practical examples further clarify how benefits-centric communication works across various domains. For instance, in a tech startup environment, demonstrating how a new application improves user experience by streamlining processes will engage investors far more effectively than detailing its programming intricacies. Similarly, in healthcare, explaining how a treatment plan enhances a patient's quality of life offers a more relatable perspective than merely discussing medical procedures.

Building Credibility and Authority

In the competitive landscape of today's professional world, establishing oneself as a credible authority is paramount to enhancing persuasive efforts. This credibility is built on several key elements that ensure your message resonates and inspires action. First and foremost, demonstrating expertise is crucial. Expertise not only enhances your reputation but also positions you as a go-to resource in your field. Sharing insights through well-recognized platforms or reputable publications can showcase your knowledge and cement your status as an authoritative figure. In doing so, your ideas gain more gravity, and people begin to look to you for guidance and solutions.

To further bolster your persuasive power, building trust is essential. Trust forms the foundation upon which relationships are built, whether with colleagues, clients, or audiences. Consistency in actions and communication paves the way for reliability, ensuring that others have confidence in your words. If your audience perceives you as dependable, they are more likely to be receptive to your ideas and suggestions. Consistency must be a hallmark of your approach—whether in delivering on promises or maintaining an unwavering commitment to your principles. As your reputation for trustworthiness solidifies, so too does your ability to influence.

Moreover, authenticity plays a vital role in establishing credibility. Being genuine and transparent in sharing your experiences allows others to connect with you on a personal level. Authenticity breeds trust and encourages alignment between you and your audience. When people sense that you are true to yourself and honest in your communications, they are more inclined to listen and believe in what you have to say. Sharing your journey, including triumphs and setbacks, reveals your human side and builds stronger connections with your audience.

Vulnerability, often underestimated, can be an empowering tool for leaders. By embracing and acknowledging your vulnerabilities, you demonstrate relatability, fostering a sense of shared humanity with those you aim to inspire. Vulnerability doesn't mean exposing every flaw; rather, it involves admitting when you don't have all the answers or sharing lessons learned from past mistakes. This transparency enhances your authority, as people are more likely to resonate with someone who understands their struggles and has navigated similar challenges.

Complementing these foundational elements, engaging in strategic content creation can significantly elevate your credibility. Creating high-quality content that offers value and addresses industry challenges can establish you as a thought leader. It's important to focus on producing actionable tips and solutions that your audience finds useful. This not only reinforces your expertise but also reinforces your commitment to helping others succeed. To achieve this, consider a checklist approach that ensures your content remains valuable and resonant over time:

1. **Identify Your Audience's Needs**: Understand who your audience is and what they seek from your expertise. Tailor your content to address their specific pain points and expectations.

2. **Provide Actionable Solutions**: Offer clear, step-by-step guidance that your audience can immediately implement. This establishes you as a problem-solver, adding to your credibility.

3. **Stay Relevant**: Regularly update your content to reflect current trends and innovations within your field. Show that you are constantly learning and adapting to new information.

4. **Incorporate Case Studies and Testimonials**: Share real-life examples of how your insights have positively impacted others. This tangible evidence further validates your authority.

5. **Engage and Respond**: Be responsive to feedback and engage with your audience through comments, discussions, and social interactions. Demonstrating attentiveness fosters trust and shows you value their opinions.

Networking with industry experts and building strong relationships can also enhance your credibility. Collaboration with knowledgeable professionals allows you to access diverse perspectives and insights, enriching your own knowledge base. Engaging in forums, attending conferences, and participating in online communities helps you connect with peers and industry leaders. These interactions position you as a well-rounded authority and open opportunities for further growth and influence.

Final Thoughts

As this chapter has shown, mastering effective persuasion techniques is essential for young professionals, mid-career individuals, and aspiring leaders aiming to enhance their leadership capabilities. By understanding and applying the principles of reciprocity and consistency, individuals can cultivate a strong ability to influence others positively. Reciprocity encourages acts of kindness and cooperation, creating environments rooted in mutual respect and collaboration. Consistency, on the other hand, taps into people's desire to align with their commitments, fostering reliable relationships and sustained motivation. Together, these principles offer powerful tools for engaging audiences and inspiring action.

By adopting a benefits-focused approach, we can further refine our persuasive skills. Emphasizing how ideas and contributions bring tangible value can set individuals apart in competitive settings. The focus on benefits rather than just features resonates deeply with audiences, whether they are colleagues, clients, or customers. This strategy not only strengthens communication and engagement but also nurtures trust and credibility. Ultimately, applying these insights helps create meaningful and enduring connections, laying the groundwork for success in both personal growth and professional endeavors.

Chapter 12

Maintaining Consistency and Momentum

Excellence is the result of daily habits that build momentum and motivation, reminding us that it's not merely about having the right opportunities but about skillfully handling them with consistent effort. If you don't find opportunities, let's create them.

- The Author

Imagine yourself riding a bicycle; once you're in motion, it's easier to pedal along, but if you stop to fix your hair, you might just end up spilling your coffee all over yourself!

Maintaining consistency and momentum is essential for progress, especially when pursuing long-term goals. This chapter explores the connection between sustained consistency and the momentum it generates. To pique interest, we delve into how maintaining steady effort can propel individuals toward achieving their aspirations. By examining practical strategies and insights, readers will gain a clearer understanding of how to harness the power of consistent actions. An exploration of these techniques offers valuable guidance for those who aim to turn routine tasks into meaningful rituals that foster personal and professional growth.

Within this chapter, we will encounter various concepts aimed at bolstering momentum through consistency. The narrative unfolds by examining the purposeful integration of daily rituals that have the potential to transform ordinary routines. These interventions serve as catalysts, generating the energy and direction needed to achieve goals. We will be introduced to the practice of self-reflection and ritual establishment, highlighting their importance in creating habits that align with long-term objectives. A careful assessment of the role intentionality plays in elevating mundane actions into powerful tools will help clarify how such practices steer individuals toward success. By addressing the significance of flexibility and personalized approaches, the chapter seeks to empower you with the confidence to adapt your strategies to meet unique challenges. Overall, this chapter aims to offer an intricate blend of theoretical insights and actionable advice, equipping you with the necessary framework to remain dedicated and driven in your pursuits.

Establishing Rituals to Maintain Direction

Integrating rituals into daily life is a powerful strategy for enhancing focus and persistence toward achieving goals. The distinction between routine and ritual lies in the intention behind the actions. Rituals have an elevated significance, infusing regular tasks with purpose and emotional resonance. For those poised to advance in their careers or leadership journeys, developing these meaningful habits can create a solid foundation for consistency and success.

A highly effective ritual to integrate into one's daily schedule is the morning check-in. This involves setting aside a brief period each morning to review and reaffirm daily objectives. A clear understanding of what needs to be accomplished sets a positive tone for the day and fosters accountability. This habit encourages individuals to align their actions with their long-term goals, creating momentum towards consistent progress. By thoughtfully planning one's day, professionals can prioritize tasks that are not only urgent but also important for advancement, mitigating distractions and maximizing productivity.

To complement the start of the day, implementing an end-of-day reflection offers significant benefits. This nightly routine serves as an opportunity to evaluate daily achievements and challenges. Taking time to assess what went well and identifying areas for improvement drives motivation and self-improvement. Reflective practices at the day's close help solidify learning experiences and encourage adaptive strategies for overcoming obstacles encountered throughout the day. Such a practice not only enhances personal growth but also builds resilience, ensuring that setbacks are viewed as opportunities for development rather than insurmountable failures.

Mindfulness practices further support these rituals by enhancing emotional awareness and resilience. Integrating mindfulness techniques, such as meditation, deep breathing, or mindful walking, into one's routine helps cultivate a state of presence and emotional clarity. This heightened awareness enables individuals to handle stress more effectively, fostering the emotional discipline necessary for sustained focus on goals. Mindfulness shifts the mind's perspective from reactive to proactive, preparing young professionals and entrepreneurs to navigate challenging situations with poise and intentionality. As my experience and studies suggest, practicing mindfulness regularly increases one's ability to maintain concentration.

Celebratory rituals provide an additional layer of motivation by acknowledging small milestones along the journey toward larger goals. Recognizing and rewarding achievements fuels enthusiasm and reinforces the behaviors required for ongoing success. These rewards need not be extravagant; simple activities, such as enjoying a favorite meal, spending time with loved ones, or indulging in a leisure activity, can serve as effective incentives. Celebrating victories builds a culture of positivity and satisfaction, encouraging continued effort and perseverance in goal pursuit.

For young professionals entering the workforce, integrating these rituals can set a strong precedence for managing responsibilities and excelling in competitive environments. Similarly, mid-career individuals seeking growth and renewed motivation benefit from structuring their day with purposeful actions that align with their career aspirations. Entrepreneurs and aspiring leaders can leverage rituals to instill principles and practices within their teams, fostering a harmonious and productive workplace culture.

While establishing rituals, it's important to keep them flexible and tailored to current personal needs. Allowing room for adjustments helps individuals adapt to unforeseen circumstances without losing sight of their goals. A rigid structure can become a source of frustration when disrupted, whereas flexibility facilitates resilience and adaptability. Exploring different activities within each ritual ensures they remain engaging and supportive of evolving objectives. Tailoring rituals to individual preferences increases their efficacy, as individuals are more likely to stay committed to a practice that resonates with their values and lifestyle preferences.

Creating a personalized morning framework often begins with self-reflection to identify core values and align activities accordingly. This could involve dedicating time to physical exercise, creative endeavors, or quiet contemplation, depending on what energizes and inspires the individual. Experimentation with various components of daily rituals over time allows individuals to discover the ideal balance that promotes both productivity and fulfillment. Moreover, maintaining openness to change ensures these rituals continue to meet the diverse demands of professional and personal development.

Intentionality is key to transforming routines into impactful rituals. By adding meaning to daily actions, individuals transcend habitual behavior, embracing a mindset conducive to achieving long-term aspirations. Establishing rituals is not merely about adherence to a strict schedule but about embedding a sense of purpose into daily life, propelling individuals toward extraordinary accomplishments.

Rewarding Progress to Reinforce Behavior

In the pursuit of long-term goals, maintaining a steady pace and consistent effort can be challenging. One method to ensure ongoing commitment is through rewarding oneself. Rewards have a profound impact on motivation and can lead to sustained effort, ultimately promoting excellence in personal and professional endeavors. By understanding and implementing strategic incentives, individuals empower themselves to stay focused and driven.

To start, it's essential to identify personal motivations and set tangible rewards that align with these desires. This process begins with a deep introspection to understand what truly matters. Are there specific leisure activities you crave or milestones you wish to celebrate? Once motivations are identified, the next step is to establish clear criteria for when rewards should be given. For instance, completing a significant project might warrant a relaxing weekend getaway, while smaller achievements could be marked by an evening off. Structuring rewards to match the magnitude of the accomplishment not only fuels progress but also enhances satisfaction. A well-defined reward system provides a framework to track progress and reinforce the connection between effort and achievement.

While initial motivations can drive action, consistently celebrating successes through positive reinforcement solidifies desired behaviors over time. Positive reinforcement involves acknowledging each success, however small, which boosts morale and strengthens the resolve to continue. Celebrations do not need to be grand; sometimes, a simple pat on the back or verbal recognition among peers suffices. By doing so, one reinforces intrinsic motivation, cultivating a mindset where discipline and achievement are inherently valuable. Offering praise and recognizing progress encourages a focus on growth rather than perfection, nudging individuals to appreciate their journey and the efforts along the way.

Finding joy in the process is equally crucial. Often, people fixate on the end goal, neglecting the importance of the steps leading up to it. By learning to enjoy small victories, individuals experience the journey as rewarding in itself. Developing this perspective alleviates the fear of failure since each step forward is celebrated regardless of the final outcome. This approach invites a growth mindset, where the process of learning and improving becomes meaningful. Joy in the journey fosters resilience, making setbacks seem less daunting because they become part of a larger, enjoyable narrative.

Accountability systems can further enhance commitment to goals by providing external support and encouragement. Setting up accountability partners creates a mutual environment of responsibility. These partnerships involve regular check-ins and shared progress updates, forming a collective goal environment where all parties benefit from each other's successes. The concept works best when both parties agree on mutual rewards—celebrating achievements together amplifies the sense of accomplishment and reinforces the social bonds necessary for sustained effort. Through accountability, individuals are less likely to lose momentum, as they are encouraged by someone who is equally invested in their growth.

Creating accountability does not require elaborate systems; it can be as simple as having a friend or colleague remind you of your commitments or share in the rewards. For entrepreneurs and aspiring leaders, this principle can extend to team settings, where shared goals foster collaboration and mutual success. Establishing these systems requires openness and trust, ensuring each party respects the other's journey while providing constructive feedback and encouragement.

Employing these strategies effectively necessitates flexibility and adaptability. As motivations evolve, so should the reward systems supporting them. Regularly reassessing what drives us prevents stagnation, allowing for dynamic adjustments that keep pursuits fresh and exciting. It's important to remember that self-reward and acknowledgment aren't about indulgence but about nurturing a thriving relationship with oneself. By choosing incentives that also appeal to personal interests and passions, people create stronger motivators aligned with intrinsic values. Experimentation is key; trying different types of rewards reveals what resonates most, tailoring approaches to individual preferences.

Over time, the practice of rewarding oneself transforms into a powerful tool for personal development and leadership. Young professionals, for instance, may find that linking incentives to career milestones encourages proactive skill development and risk-taking, enhancing their competitive edge in the workplace. Mid-career individuals seeking transformation might use incentives to reignite passion and drive, shifting focus towards new challenges and growth opportunities. Entrepreneurs, meanwhile, can incorporate these principles into their business cultures, establishing environments where employees feel valued and motivated to excel.

Evaluating and Refining Approaches Regularly

In the pursuit of long-term goals, maintaining consistency and momentum is critical. Yet, to ensure this forward motion is effective, periodic evaluation and adaptation are necessary. As we navigate the path toward achieving our objectives, taking a moment to assess our strategies can make all the difference in staying on course.

Conducting regular self-assessments is the first step in this journey. These evaluations provide an opportunity to reflect on your progress, identify areas that may need adjustment, and engage more actively in the goal-setting process. For instance, imagine setting a goal to improve your public speaking skills. Initially, you might measure success by how you feel after each presentation, but over time, you could refine this by recording your speeches and analyzing them for clarity and impact. This ongoing assessment helps pinpoint what needs improvement and highlights what strategies work best for you.

To complement self-assessment, adopting flexibility in plans is essential. Life often throws unexpected challenges and opportunities our way, and being rigid can impede progress. An agile mindset allows for real-time course corrections, enabling you to pivot when necessary without losing sight of your ultimate objective. For example, if you're an entrepreneur with a business plan set in stone, you might miss out on new market trends. By being open to change, you can explore these opportunities, potentially tapping into unanticipated sources of growth. This doesn't mean abandoning initial goals but rather adjusting pathways to achieve them more effectively.

Seeking feedback from external sources is another crucial aspect of maintaining momentum. Gathering insights from others can illuminate blind spots and accelerate your growth. This means actively inviting opinions from colleagues, mentors, or even your team and using their perspectives to build a more comprehensive view of your progress. A software developer, for example, could benefit from peer reviews of their code, which may reveal inefficiencies they hadn't noticed themselves. Such feedback loops foster learning and innovation, ultimately leading to stronger outcomes.

Equally important is journaling your progress. Keeping a detailed account of your experiences not only provides clarity but also serves as tangible evidence of your growth over time. Through journaling, you can look back at past entries and see how far you've come, which can be incredibly motivating. Suppose you're a mid-career professional seeking transformation. Regularly documenting thoughts about your challenges and successes can help identify patterns in your behavior and reactions, offering insights into what drives your productivity and satisfaction. This reflection not only encourages personal growth but also helps refine strategies moving forward.

Guidelines for these practices can ensure they become integrated parts of your routine. For self-assessment, set specific intervals, such as monthly or quarterly, for evaluating different aspects of your progress, whether in skill acquisition or emotional resilience. When it comes to journaling, establish a habit, perhaps writing weekly entries that summarize achievements, lessons learned, and adjustments needed. These structured approaches transform abstract intentions into concrete actions, making it easier to stay consistent.

While it's tempting to stick to a predetermined path, especially when starting out, recognizing the value of evaluation and adaptation is key to sustaining momentum. Each strategy—whether self-assessment, flexibility, feedback, or journaling—plays a vital role in building the resilience required to achieve long-term success. As young professionals enter the workforce, embracing these practices will aid in establishing careers and enhancing leadership skills. Mid-career individuals will find them invaluable for breaking through stagnation and reigniting motivation. Entrepreneurs, meanwhile, can use these tools to foster ethical, effective business practices, empowering both themselves and their teams.

Summary and Reflections

Throughout this chapter, we've explored how integrating rituals into daily routines can significantly impact both personal and professional growth. By establishing intentional habits like morning check-ins and end-of-day reflections, individuals create a framework for consistency that propels them toward their long-term goals. These practices not only help maintain focus but also enhance resilience in the face of challenges. Mindfulness techniques add an extra layer of emotional awareness, enabling professionals to navigate stress with greater ease. Additionally, celebratory rituals reinforce positive behavior by acknowledging progress, thereby sustaining momentum and motivation.

By applying these principles, young professionals can lay a strong foundation for successful careers, while mid-career individuals and entrepreneurs can find renewed energy and purpose in their work. It's important to tailor these rituals to fit personal needs, ensuring they remain flexible and adaptable to life's changes. Regularly evaluating one's approach further guarantees that efforts align with evolving aspirations. Ultimately, these rituals are about embedding meaning into everyday actions, transforming routines into powerful tools for achievement and paving the way toward extraordinary accomplishments.

Chapter 13

The Synergy of Team Collaboration

T.E.A.M. Together, Everybody Achieves More; through collaboration, we tap into collective wisdom, and teamwork becomes the secret ingredient that transforms ordinary efforts into extraordinary results. **- The Author**

Imagine yourself baking a cake; each team member is an ingredient—flour, sugar, eggs—and together, when mixed with a dash of humor and a sprinkle of support, you create a delicious masterpiece that no one could whip up alone!

The synergy of team collaboration lies at the heart of achieving enhanced outcomes and mutual growth, offering a pathway for both personal development and organizational success. Across diverse professional landscapes, the ability to work cohesively as a group can transform individual efforts into powerful collective achievements. This chapter explores the intricate dynamics of teamwork, where collaborative efforts not only amplify productivity but also nurture a culture that values every member's input. Understanding how to harness these dynamics is crucial for individuals seeking to excel in competitive environments, whether they are just entering the workforce or looking to rejuvenate their career paths.

Throughout this chapter, we will uncover strategies for fostering open communication within teams, ensuring each voice is heard without fear of judgment. It will discuss how aligning team goals with individual strengths boosts morale and efficiency, highlighting the importance of recognizing personal abilities for task delegation. Furthermore, the chapter delves into managing conflicts constructively, showing how resolving disputes can fortify relationships rather than weaken them. By learning from past conflicts and employing structured conflict resolution techniques, teams can create resilient, supportive environments. Through these discussions, the chapter aims to provide practical insights and tools for young professionals, mid-career individuals, entrepreneurs, and aspiring leaders to cultivate effective, respectful, and inclusive workplaces.

Fostering the Culture of Open Communication

Promoting an environment where team members feel safe to share ideas and feedback is the foundation of effective collaboration and innovation. Creating such a culture requires intentional efforts to establish psychological safety, which can lead to improved outcomes for both individuals and the team as a whole.

One way to foster this environment is by establishing specific areas and times for open discussions. These dedicated spaces provide team members with opportunities to express their thoughts freely without fear of retribution or judgment. Regularly scheduled meetings or brainstorming sessions can serve as platforms for these dialogues, ensuring that everyone knows when their voice can be heard. By setting aside time for these exchanges, teams create safe spaces that encourage all members to contribute, regardless of their position or seniority.

Open communication is crucial in building trust within a team. When individuals are encouraged to speak openly and honestly, trust naturally develops among team members. This trust fosters more authentic relationships, as people feel comfortable sharing their insights and feedback. A team that communicates transparently is better equipped to address challenges and leverage each member's strengths effectively. Trust transforms interactions from transactional to genuine, creating a cohesive and unified group focused on achieving shared goals.

Furthermore, creativity thrives in environments where individuals feel heard and valued. When team members know that their ideas will be considered seriously, they are more likely to engage actively and bring creative solutions to the table. This sense of being valued not only enhances individual productivity but also boosts overall team engagement. Encouraging diverse perspectives ensures a wide range of innovative approaches, enriching the team's problem-solving capabilities. Diverse teams with open channels for idea-sharing often outperform those that lack such inclusivity, as they can draw upon a vast reservoir of knowledge and inspiration.

Regular check-ins are another vital component of promoting transparency and fostering continuous project feedback. These check-ins provide a structured opportunity for team members to update one another on progress, discuss any obstacles, and receive constructive feedback. By incorporating regular intervals for reflection and dialogue, teams maintain alignment with their objectives and can make necessary adjustments in real-time. Furthermore, these check-ins cultivate a culture of accountability, as individuals are expected to share updates and contribute to the team's collective understanding of project status.

Establishing guidelines around these check-ins can further enhance their effectiveness. For instance, setting clear expectations about the frequency and structure of these meetings ensures consistent participation and preparation from all members. Providing a framework for giving and receiving feedback can also enhance the quality of these discussions, focusing on growth rather than criticism. Feedback loops established through regular check-ins promote a culture of continuous improvement, enabling teams to adapt swiftly to changing circumstances and seize new opportunities.

By valuing each member's contributions and promoting active participation, teams can overcome barriers to collaboration and unlock the full potential of their collective talents. Encouraging everyone to share their insights and experiences creates a rich tapestry of ideas that can drive innovation and propel the team forward. Teams should strive to affirm the importance of every voice, ensuring that all individuals feel empowered to contribute meaningfully to discussions and decisions.

Creating a culture where psychological safety thrives requires ongoing commitment and effort. Leaders play a critical role in championing this culture by modeling open communication, recognizing and celebrating successes, and supporting team members in expressing themselves freely. When leaders dedicate themselves to nurturing an inclusive environment, they pave the way for unparalleled collaboration and growth.

Aligning Team Goals with Individual Strengths

Recognizing individual strengths within a team is a crucial step towards achieving synchronized team objectives. By identifying specific skills and abilities, leaders can allocate tasks that align with each member's capabilities, thereby enhancing effectiveness. This strategic delegation not only ensures that the right people are working on tasks suited to their talents but also boosts morale and engagement as individuals feel valued and understood in their roles. For instance, a team member with strong analytical skills will thrive when given data-driven projects, while someone with exceptional creativity might excel in roles requiring innovative solutions.

Setting goals that reflect the strengths of each team member is essential for maximizing potential and success. When personal talents are harnessed effectively, individuals can contribute more productively toward team objectives. This alignment creates a sense of ownership and responsibility, as team members work towards goals they are naturally equipped to achieve. Moreover, it cultivates a motivating work environment where everyone is challenged yet confident in their ability to meet these challenges. Consider a marketing team tasked with launching a new product: assigning roles based on strengths—such as a copywriter focusing on content creation and a strategist on campaign planning—ensures smooth execution and optimizes results.

Team-building exercises are valuable tools for highlighting individual strengths and fostering trust and teamwork. These activities provide opportunities for members to step outside their usual roles and showcase different skills, revealing hidden talents that can be leveraged in future projects. Furthermore, such exercises build camaraderie, breaking down barriers and encouraging open communication among the team. For example, a problem-solving challenge can highlight leadership qualities in quieter team members, while collaborative projects can bring out creative insights from unexpected sources. The trust and understanding developed through these exercises translate into more cohesive teams that perform better and communicate openly.

Creating growth plans aligned with individual aspirations and organizational objectives support continual development. It is important for organizations to recognize that personal growth contributes significantly to overall success. Growth plans should encapsulate both professional and personal goals, keeping in mind the broader objectives of the organization. By doing so, individuals are motivated to pursue their developmental paths, knowing there is room for career advancement aligned with their interests. This approach not only enhances job satisfaction but also ensures that employees remain engaged and committed to the organization's mission.

A practical guideline for identifying individual strengths involves conducting regular assessments and feedback sessions. These can be structured meetings or informal discussions where team members share their experiences and insights about their roles. Encouragement from leaders to self-reflect and identify areas where they excel can further empower individuals. Moreover, utilizing tools such as strength assessments or personality tests can provide additional clarity and serve as a foundation for effective task delegation.

When setting complementary goals, it is pivotal to engage in collaborative goal-setting processes. This means involving the team in discussions about their aims and how these align with the larger organizational strategy. By inviting input, leaders can ensure that goals are realistic and attainable within the team's collective skill set. Open dialogue allows for adjustments and encourages buy-in, making it more likely for goals to be embraced and pursued passionately.

Facilitating team-building exercises requires thoughtful planning to ensure inclusivity and relevance. Activities should be designed to reflect real-world scenarios that the team may encounter, bridging the gap between practice and application. Leaders should aim to create environments where all members feel comfortable participating and expressing themselves. Successful exercises result in heightened team spirit and an improved understanding of individual contributions to group dynamics.

Finally, growth plans need to be comprehensive and tailored. This begins with clear communication between managers and employees to ascertain personal ambitions and how they can be interwoven with company needs. Regular check-ins provide opportunities to review progress and make necessary adjustments, ensuring alignment remains intact. Personal development workshops and training programs can be integrated into these plans, offering continuous learning and adaptability.

Managing Conflicts Constructively

Addressing and resolving conflicts in a manner that strengthens relationships and fosters cooperation is crucial for effective team collaboration. Recognizing conflict as normal encourages proactive approaches before issues escalate, which is vital for maintaining a harmonious work environment. Conflict is an inevitable part of any team dynamic, and acknowledging it as a natural occurrence can shift our perspective on how to deal with it. When seen as a potential for growth rather than a roadblock, conflicts can be managed more effectively, leading to better outcomes for all parties involved.

Utilizing structured conflict resolution techniques ensures fair and respectful outcomes. These techniques, such as mediation and negotiation, provide frameworks for resolving disagreements in a way that respects each individual's perspective while aiming for a win-win situation. Implementing these techniques requires setting up guidelines to ensure that conversations are constructive. For example, active listening is a key component of successful conflict resolution, allowing team members to feel heard and understood, which increases mutual respect and understanding. Structured methods provide a safe space where individuals can express their viewpoints without fear of retaliation or dismissal.

Empowering team members to resolve their conflicts develops interpersonal skills and resilience. When individuals take responsibility for resolving their disputes, they gain valuable experience in communication and problem-solving. This empowerment not only boosts confidence but also enhances the overall resilience of the team—members to become more adept at handling future conflicts independently. Providing training in conflict management can equip team members with the necessary skills to handle disagreements constructively.

Learning from conflicts enhances team dynamics and problem-solving skills for future interactions. Each conflict serves as a learning opportunity, offering insights into the underlying issues within a team's processes or relationships. By reflecting on these instances, teams can identify patterns that may lead to disputes and address them proactively. This learning process promotes continuous improvement in team dynamics, fostering a culture of open communication and adaptability.

In practice, recognizing conflicts early on allows team members to engage in open dialogues before tensions rise. These conversations are most effective when facilitated in an environment that prioritizes inclusivity and mutual respect. Encouraging open dialogue not only helps with diffusing tension but also offers opportunities to reinforce team values such as trust and collaboration. Managers and leaders play a crucial role here by modeling effective conflict resolution behavior. They set the tone for how conflicts are perceived and managed within the team, guiding employees towards solutions that benefit everyone involved.

Structured conflict resolution techniques like mediation often involve bringing conflicting parties together to discuss their grievances openly. Mediators act as neutral parties that help guide the conversation towards productive outcomes. This method emphasizes problem-solving over blame-assigning, ensuring that all voices are heard, and consensus is reached amicably.

Overall, structured approaches facilitate a peaceful resolution, preserving and often strengthening working relationships.

Empowering team members to tackle their own conflicts encourages personal and professional growth. This autonomy in conflict management cultivates a sense of ownership and accountability among team members. They learn to assess situations critically, consider multiple perspectives, and negotiate solutions that are mutually beneficial. As a result, employees develop stronger interpersonal skills that contribute positively to both their careers and personal lives.

Additionally, learning from past conflicts provides essential lessons for improving team functionality. Teams can conduct debriefings after conflicts to discuss what worked well and what could have been handled differently. This reflective practice not only improves current processes but also equips the team with strategies to prevent similar issues in the future. By examining conflicts analytically, teams transform potentially negative experiences into catalysts for growth and innovation.

Insights and Implications

In this chapter, we explored the significance of creating an environment that nurtures open communication and psychological safety within teams. By establishing dedicated spaces for dialogue and encouraging transparency, teams can cultivate trust and build more authentic relationships among members. The chapter highlighted how these practices not only enhance creativity and productivity but also allow team members to share diverse perspectives, thus enriching problem-solving capabilities. This emphasis on inclusivity ensures that every voice is heard, fostering a collaborative spirit where challenges are addressed effectively, and collective strengths are harnessed.

Additionally, recognizing and aligning individual strengths with team goals emerged as a vital component in achieving shared objectives. Through strategic delegation and embracing personal talents, teams can boost morale and engagement while executing tasks more efficiently. Team-building exercises and regular check-ins were identified as effective tools for promoting understanding and continuous improvement. These strategies empower individuals by providing avenues for growth and enabling them to contribute meaningfully. As team dynamics evolve, employing structured conflict resolution techniques further strengthens relationships, allowing teams to overcome obstacles constructively. Emphasizing these collaborative efforts ultimately leads to enhanced outcomes and mutual growth for all involved.

Chapter 14

Developing Unwavering Persistence

Success and failure are merely steppingstones on the path of unwavering persistence; it's the courage to keep going, the determination to linger longer with challenges, and the resilience gained through overcoming difficulties that truly define our journey.

- The Author

Imagine yourself trying to teach a dog to fetch the ball; it may take a few dozen throws and more than a few failed attempts, but with every repetition, you both get better, and eventually, you'll have a furry friend that won't quit until the ball is retrieved (or at least until snack time)!

Developing unwavering persistence is central to navigating life's challenges and achieving success in personal and professional realms. Persistence acts as the backbone of resilience, enabling individuals to push through obstacles rather than retreat at the first sign of adversity. This chapter delves into how a consistent application of persistence can transform daunting challenges into manageable achievements. It also explores the mental fortitude required to maintain focus over time, despite setbacks or distractions. For young professionals, mid-career individuals, and aspiring leaders alike, nurturing this tenacity becomes an essential part of their journey toward fulfillment and excellence.

In this chapter, we will learn about practical strategies and techniques for building persistence by breaking down large goals into manageable steps. The narrative unfolds with a focus on simplifying ambitious objectives, making them less intimidating and more achievable. You are introduced to methods such as chunking, which involves dividing significant goals into smaller tasks, thereby enhancing motivation and clarity. Techniques like milestone mapping are discussed, offering insights into creating timelines that ensure steady progress while maintaining momentum. Additionally, the importance of celebrating small victories is highlighted, reinforcing positive behaviors and sustaining enthusiasm. Through this comprehensive exploration, you will gain valuable tools to cultivate persistence, ultimately turning obstacles into steppingstones on their path to success.

Breaking Down Large Goals into Manageable Steps

Breaking down big goals into achievable chunks is crucial in the path to unwavering persistence. When faced with daunting objectives, it is essential to simplify them into smaller, more manageable tasks—a strategy known as chunking. This approach not only reduces feelings of overwhelm but also provides a clearer focus, making the journey toward success more tangible. Chunking for success involves dividing a large goal into smaller, actionable steps. By doing so, these steps become less intimidating and significantly increase motivation. For instance, if a young professional aims to attain a promotion within a company, this overarching ambition might feel overwhelming. However, by breaking it down into smaller tasks—such as completing specific projects, acquiring new skills, or networking with colleagues—it becomes more feasible and easier to tackle. Each completed task serves as a building block towards achieving the larger objective.

Milestone mapping is another vital technique in turning grand visions into reality. This method involves creating a timeline with specific deadlines for each mini-goal. Not only does this structure allow for better organization, but it also helps maintain momentum throughout the journey. A timeline acts as a roadmap, ensuring that progress is consistently tracked, and adjustments can be made when necessary. Aspire to set milestones that are realistic and attainable within a specified timeframe. For mid-career individuals seeking transformation, milestone mapping can prop up motivation levels by providing clear checkpoints along their career growth path. A concise timeline enables them to stay focused, eliminating distractions and maintaining a steady pace towards their ultimate goal.

Celebrating small wins is equally important in maintaining enthusiasm and reinforcing positive behavior. Each mini-goal accomplished should be acknowledged and celebrated as a victory. These celebrations act as motivational boosts, injecting a sense of accomplishment and encouraging further progress. For example, entrepreneurs often recognize and reward their teams for reaching business milestones, such as completing a successful product launch or surpassing sales targets. Such acknowledgments cultivate a culture of positivity and achievement within the workplace, fostering an environment in which persistence thrives.

Reflective practices play a significant role in developing unwavering persistence through self-awareness and resilience. Regular reflection allows individuals to evaluate their progress, assess any deviations from their planned trajectory, and make necessary adjustments. It offers a moment of introspection, granting clarity on what strategies work and which ones require modification. For aspiring leaders, reflecting periodically on their leadership style, communication skills, and decision-making processes can guide their evolution into more effective and empathetic leaders. The ability to adapt and learn from past experiences is a hallmark of resilient individuals who persist despite challenges.

Guided by these principles, the process of simplifying big goals becomes less about the magnitude of the objective and more about the methodical steps taken to achieve it. Incorporating these strategies requires consistency, discipline, and an open mindset willing to embrace change and uncertainty. In essence, cultivating persistence is not solely about reaching the end goal; it is about embracing the journey, learning along the way, and growing stronger with every setback encountered.

For those entering the workforce, understanding how to break down ambitious career goals can be pivotal in establishing a solid foundation for future success. By mastering the art of chunking, milestone mapping, celebrating small wins, and practicing reflection, young professionals equip themselves with valuable tools that enhance both personal and professional growth. They learn to navigate complex environments with confidence, transforming obstacles into steppingstones.

Similarly, mid-career individuals benefit from these methods as they strive for renewed motivation and career advancement. In competitive settings, the ability to simplify goals lends clarity and direction to their pursuits, enabling them to outperform stagnation and ignite their passion for growth. Entrepreneurs and leaders, too, harness the power of these techniques to foster productive workplaces where innovation and perseverance flourishes.

Visualizing Success to Stay Motivated

Visualization, a powerful tool in personal development, serves as a crucial motivator for cultivating persistence. By vividly picturing goals and aspirations, individuals can harness this mental practice to bolster their resolve and navigate the challenges on the path to success. This section explores various visualization techniques that serve as catalysts for developing unwavering persistence.

Creating a vision board is a compelling way to keep your goals front and center. This tangible representation of aspirations acts as a continuous reminder of what you're striving for, reinforcing commitment every time you glance at it. A vision board is not just a collection of pictures; it's a personal roadmap peppered with images and words that resonate with your deepest desires. For young professionals launching their careers, a vision board can anchor their ambitions amidst the many distractions of modern life, serving as a daily dose of inspiration. It's a simple yet effective method to ensure that one's dreams are never far from sight, providing motivation to pursue them relentlessly. To craft an impactful vision board, start by identifying your core goals and aspirations. Gather images, quotes, or objects that symbolize these targets. Arrange these elements on a board or digital platform where you'll see them regularly. Allow flexibility for updates as goals evolve. This exercise not only helps clarify objectives but also infuses daily life with purpose and direction.

Moving beyond physical representations, mental imagery techniques focus on the mind's power to visualize success. These exercises involve closing your eyes and vividly imagining the successful outcomes of your efforts. Imagine the sensations associated with achieving a long-term goal — the sights, sounds, and even smells. Engaging in such detailed mental rehearsal can ignite immediate motivation, providing a burst of clarity when tasks seem overwhelming. Visualization isn't limited to athletes or performers; it's beneficial for anyone seeking to enhance their clarity of purpose and maintain focus despite distractions. This technique not only strengthens the mental impression of future success but also encourages action towards making that vision a reality.

Incorporating visualization into daily routines can be transformative. As with any skill, consistency is key to deriving its benefits fully. Regularly dedicating time to visualize goals reinforces a positive mindset and aids in overcoming discouragement. Imagine starting each day with a few minutes of peaceful visualization, setting the tone for productivity and focus. For mid-career individuals feeling stagnant, integrating such a routine can rejuvenate passion and drive. It not only maintains the momentum necessary to push through obstacles but also fosters resilience. Consider pairing this practice with morning or evening rituals, ensuring that visualization becomes as integral to your day as checking emails or preparing meals. Over time, this consistent engagement with your goals can create a sustained sense of achievement and progression.

A significant aspect of visualization lies in harnessing emotions tied to goals. An emotional connection to one's aspirations not only deepens commitment but also fortifies resilience during challenging times. When you visualize your journey, consider the emotions linked to each milestone. Feel the excitement of success and let it fuel your perseverance. Emotions play a vital role in shaping our responses to adversity. By consciously associating positive feelings with your goals, you build a robust emotional foundation that supports persistence. Entrepreneurs and aspiring leaders, often navigating unpredictable landscapes, can leverage this emotional aspect to stay committed, turning challenges into opportunities for growth.

To illustrate visualization's power, countless success stories underline its effectiveness. Elite athletes visualizing their performance, entrepreneurs envisioning business milestones, and artists imagining their masterpieces all demonstrate how this mental practice translates into real-world achievement. The common thread among these examples is the unwavering belief that if one can conceive it mentally, they can achieve it physically. Visualization acts as a bridge between the present and the desired future, offering a safe space to practice resilience before facing real-life hurdles.

While visualization is a formidable tool, it's most effective when complemented by action. Seeing a future vision can significantly boost motivation, yet the path to realization involves taking concrete steps. Thus, while visualization fuels the journey, practical efforts ensure progression. Use your mental images as blueprints, guiding decisions and actions toward fulfilling those visions. Persistence is born out of the synergy between imagination and execution, turning abstract dreams into tangible realities.

Using Grit as a Tool for Progression

To fully appreciate the role of grit in fostering persistence, it's essential to first define and understand this powerful trait. At its core, grit involves perseverance and passion for long-term goals. Unlike mere talent or intelligence, which are often viewed as fixed attributes, grit is about maintaining effort over an extended period regardless of obstacles or setbacks. This quality forms a critical foundation for both personal and professional growth.

My research and experience as the CEO of a large high-tech awarded company on grit highlights its importance as a significant predictor of success. My research (over 8 editions of my 3 Days Course "Being Excellent", since 2010) demonstrates that individuals with high levels of grit tend to outperform those who rely solely on natural talent. The reason is simple: while talent can provide a head start, it is perseverance and passion that sustain the journey over the long haul.

Consider the story of Albert Einstein, who is famously quoted as saying, "It's not that I'm so smart, it's just that I stay with problems longer." Einstein's success didn't stem from his intelligence alone but from his relentless tenacity and passion for unraveling complex questions. His journey exemplifies the power of grit—it's not only about pushing through difficulties but also about continuously nurturing a deep interest in one's pursuits.

The concept of grit can often be misunderstood as sheer persistence separated from a genuine emotional connection to one's goals. However, to cultivate authentic grit, passion must play a crucial role. Passion fuels the drive to persist by imbuing tasks with meaning and joy. Without passion, persistence might still lead to achievement, yet it lacks satisfaction and can lead to burnout or stress.

Let's explore strategies for cultivating grit effectively. One practical approach is setting long-term goals accompanied by short-term objectives. These provide a clear roadmap and allow for measurable progress, reinforcing motivation as milestones are achieved. For young professionals entering the workforce, establishing specific career targets and benchmarks helps maintain focus in competitive environments. Mid-career individuals can rejuvenate their paths by identifying fresh ambitions that align with their evolving interests and skills.

In addition to goal setting, developing a growth mindset is vital—a belief that abilities and talents can be cultivated through dedication and hard work. This mindset shifts the perception of setbacks from insurmountable barriers to opportunities for growth and learning. By embracing challenges and recognizing the value of constructive feedback, individuals enhance their grit and persistence organically.

For entrepreneurs and aspiring leaders, intertwining passion with purpose serves as a catalyst for sustaining grit. When business ventures align with personal values and aspirations, they generate enthusiasm and a resilient spirit. This alignment not only propels leaders forward but also inspires teams to share in the collective vision.

Another effective strategy for nurturing grit involves deliberate practice. This entails engaging in focused, repetitive efforts to hone skills while refining processes. Through deliberate practice, both entrepreneurs and professionals can build expertise and confidence, making daunting tasks more manageable and less intimidating.

Furthermore, passion-driven grit fosters a positive outlook on overcoming obstacles. Those who pursue their interests with zeal view setbacks not as threats but as steppingstones toward achieving their dreams. This positive association transforms challenges into sources of motivation rather than discouragement.

For young professionals, seeking careers that resonate with their passions not only enhances job satisfaction but also encourages resilience amid workplace challenges. Mid-career individuals can reinvigorate their professional lives by revisiting their passions and integrating them into new ventures or roles, thereby reigniting the flame of persistence.

Creating a supportive environment is another factor in fostering grit. Encouragement from peers, mentors, and managers bolsters confidence and reinforces the determination to persevere. When individuals feel backed by a community that shares their aspirations, they are more likely to remain steadfast in the face of adversity.

Lastly, maintaining an intrinsic motivation anchored in passion is crucial. While external rewards such as promotions or accolades are rewarding, internal satisfaction derived from meaningful work provides lasting fulfillment. Pursuing what genuinely excites and stimulates allows individuals to find joy in the journey itself, transforming effort into an enjoyable experience.

Concluding Thoughts

Persistence is a powerful tool that fuels progress and achievement. Throughout the chapter, various strategies emerged as essential for cultivating this trait: breaking down goals into smaller, manageable steps, setting milestones, celebrating small victories, and engaging in reflective practices. These approaches equip individuals with the clarity needed to focus on each task without feeling overwhelmed by the larger goal. Whether you are stepping into the workforce or navigating complex career stages, applying these techniques will help you develop the resilience required to transform challenges into opportunities. By nurturing persistence, you not only move closer to your objectives but also build strength through every experience.

As we navigate our careers and personal growth journeys, it's crucial to remember that success isn't solely about reaching the endpoint; it's about embracing the process and learning along the way. Persistence, honed through strategic planning and adaptability, empowers us to face obstacles with confidence. Whether you're starting out, seeking renewal, or leading others, fostering persistence enables steady progress in competitive environments. For young professionals, mid-career individuals, and entrepreneurs alike, the methods discussed provide a foundation for sustainable growth. Applying these principles can lead to fulfilling achievements that reflect both personal aspirations and professional excellence.

Chapter 15

Striking the Balance between Ambition and Well-being

While ambition sets the stage for success, it's happiness that truly unlocks our potential; by focusing our efforts wisely and proactively, we learn that the journey is just as important as the destination. **- The Author**

Imagine yourself walking a tightrope; if you're too focused on reaching the other side, you might just forget to enjoy the view—so take a moment to wave at the audience and remember to breathe along the way!

Striking the balance between ambition and well-being is fundamental to achieving real success. In a world that often celebrates relentless drive, it becomes vital to remember that sustainable achievement requires a harmonious approach to professional aspirations and personal health. Many young professionals entering the workforce are eager to make their mark, while mid-career individuals often seek growth and revitalization. Entrepreneurs, too, are driven by the desire to build impactful businesses. For all, finding the delicate equilibrium between pursuing ambitious goals and maintaining mental and physical health is not just desirable but essential. A mindful strategy that incorporates this balance ensures that the path to success does not lead to burnout or exhaustion. It invites reflection on one's priorities and encourages the pursuit of a fulfilling career without compromising well-being.

Throughout this chapter, we explore the intricate relationship between ambition and well-being, emphasizing how recognizing warning signs such as burnout can prevent personal and professional setbacks. You will be guided through the process of identifying symptoms and understanding their impact on various aspects of life. The chapter also delves into practical strategies for prioritizing health amidst ambitious pursuits, incorporating regular exercise, mindfulness practices, and sleep hygiene as pivotal components of a balanced lifestyle. Furthermore, it addresses the importance of setting realistic boundaries to protect personal space while allowing space for professional excellence. By examining these themes, the chapter aims to equip readers with tools to navigate their careers thoughtfully, ensuring that the pursuit of success aligns with maintaining a healthy and productive life. Through a narrative style, the discussion unfolds to resonate with the experiences and aspirations of diverse audiences, from the budding professional stepping onto the career ladder to the seasoned entrepreneur steering their business with purpose.

Recognizing signs of burnout

Understanding the symptoms of burnout and identifying them early on is crucial for maintaining one's well-being. Burnout is a multifaceted condition that affects individuals physically, emotionally, cognitively, and behaviorally. Recognizing these symptoms is the first step towards managing stress effectively.

Physical symptoms are often the most noticeable indicators of burnout. Fatigue is a common sign—feeling persistently tired even after adequate rest might suggest more than just a lack of sleep. Frequent headaches can also indicate stress levels have reached a tipping point. These physical signs serve as alarms, signaling that it's time to reassess workload and lifestyle choices to prevent further distress. Establishing a regular exercise routine and ensuring proper nutrition can help mitigate these symptoms.

Emotional symptoms of burnout often manifest as cynicism or irritability. Individuals experiencing burnout may become indifferent towards their responsibilities or critical of their peers. This emotional detachment can cause strain in personal and professional relationships. Developing emotional awareness is essential for navigating these feelings and maintaining healthy connections with others. Mindfulness practices, such as meditation or yoga, offer tools for recognizing and managing emotions, enabling better communication and understanding with colleagues and loved ones.

Cognitive symptoms include difficulty concentrating or making decisions due to cognitive overload. When overwhelmed, mental clarity diminishes, leading to decreased productivity and satisfaction. Taking breaks is vital; stepping away from tasks provides the brain with an opportunity to relax and reset. Simple activities like walking in nature or engaging in hobbies unrelated to work can help restore focus and creativity. Such practices counteract the cognitive weariness associated with constant stress and provide long-term benefits for mental health.

Behavioral symptoms of burnout often lead to withdrawal from social interactions, underscoring an unhealthy work-life balance. Isolation can exacerbate stress, as it deprives individuals of the support systems necessary for coping. Social connections play a pivotal role in psychological resilience. Engaging with friends, family, or even co-workers in non-work-related activities helps reinforce these bonds. Participating in group activities or simply sharing experiences with others can create a sense of belonging and community, which acts as a buffer against burnout.

Recognizing these symptoms is the first step towards addressing burnout proactively. It's important to understand that burnout doesn't arise overnight but builds up over time. Therefore, early identification of symptoms can prevent the escalation of stress and its harmful effects on both personal and professional life. Implementing small changes in daily routines, such as prioritizing self-care and setting realistic expectations, can significantly reduce the risk of burnout. Regularly checking in on one's mental state and acknowledging any warning signs ensures that steps are taken before burnout becomes overwhelming.

In addition to personal efforts, organizational support plays a significant role in preventing burnout. Work environments that promote open communication, flexible schedules, and opportunities for development can significantly alleviate stress. Encouraging employees to voice concerns and offering resources like employee assistance programs contribute to a healthier workplace culture. This collaborative approach not only boosts morale but also increases productivity and job satisfaction.

Building resilience is also an important aspect of combating burnout. Resilience involves the ability to bounce back from setbacks and adapt to challenging situations. Fostering resilience requires a combination of individual effort and environmental support. Practicing gratitude, maintaining a positive outlook, and focusing on achievable goals enhance personal strength against adversities. Meanwhile, workplaces should provide training and resources that empower individuals to manage challenges effectively.

Ultimately, understanding burnout's symptoms and implementing strategies to address them cultivates a balanced approach to ambition and well-being. Both individuals and organizations have roles to play in creating a supportive environment where people can thrive without sacrificing their mental and physical health. By adopting a proactive stance, the damaging effects of burnout can be diminished, paving the way for sustainable success and fulfillment in all aspects of life.

Prioritizing mental and physical health

In the pursuit of long-term success, prioritizing mental and physical health stands as a pillar for achieving sustainable ambition. For young professionals, mid-career individuals, and entrepreneurs alike, it is crucial to understand that success does not have to come at the expense of one's well-being. In this regard, establishing a routine that integrates regular exercise, mindfulness practices, a nutritious diet, and good sleep hygiene can pave the way for improved performance both in personal and professional arenas.

Regular exercise emerges as a powerful tool for balancing ambition with well-being. Engaging in physical activities such as running, swimming, or even brisk walking releases endorphins— natural chemicals in the body that alleviate pain and boost pleasure sensations, leading to an uplifted mood. By moving your body frequently, you not only enhance your mood but also reduce anxiety and sharpen cognitive performance. This improvement in mental faculties boosts productivity and fosters creativity, which are essential elements of sustained career growth. The benefits of exercise extend beyond mere physical fitness, making it an indispensable component of a well-rounded lifestyle.

Mindfulness practices like meditation further contribute to striking a balance between ambition and well-being. Meditation helps increase self-awareness, allowing individuals to process emotions better and respond to stress more effectively. It equips practitioners with the tools necessary for navigating the complexities of modern work environments, where emotional intelligence is increasingly valued. Through regular mindfulness exercises, one gains clarity and focus—traits that greatly enhance problem-solving skills and decision-making abilities. Simple practices like deep breathing exercises or progressive muscle relaxation can be incorporated into daily routines to foster a sense of calm and resilience.

Additionally, maintaining a nutritious diet plays a pivotal role in supporting both physical and mental health. A balanced diet rich in fruits, vegetables, whole grains, and lean proteins provides the necessary nutrients for optimal brain function. Nutritious foods fuel your body and mind, elevating energy levels and enhancing cognitive capabilities. This dietary approach ensures that you're equipped with the stamina needed to tackle challenges and pursue your goals with vigor. Consider integrating omega-3 fatty acids from fish, antioxidants from berries, and fiber from leafy greens, as these nutrients have been associated with improved memory and concentration.

Equally important is the adoption of good sleep hygiene, which serves as a catalyst for enhanced cognitive functions and overall productivity. Lack of sleep has been linked to impaired attention, slower reaction times, and reduced motivation—the very antithesis of what ambitious individuals aspire to achieve. Establishing a consistent sleep schedule and creating a restful environment can significantly improve sleep quality. Ensure your bedroom is dark, quiet, and cool, and develop a pre-sleep routine that signals your body it's time to wind down. Such practices promote restorative sleep, thereby fostering overall health and enabling you to operate at your best during waking hours.

For young professionals entering the workforce, understanding how these elements synergize can lead to successful integration into demanding roles without sacrificing personal health. By actively incorporating exercise, mindfulness, nutrition, and sleep hygiene into your lifestyle, you cultivate a foundation that supports career advancement and leadership development. Mid-career individuals may find that reviving their commitment to these health practices reinvigorates their drive and offers fresh perspectives on overcoming stagnation. A renewed focus on well-being can provide the motivation needed to power through plateaus and transition toward new opportunities.

Entrepreneurs and aspiring leaders will benefit by embedding these healthful habits not only in their lives but also in their organizational cultures. Encouraging team members to prioritize well-being creates a supportive environment where everyone is empowered to excel. Embracing holistic health practices within a business setting can lead to increased employee satisfaction, reduced burnout, and enhanced team performance, all of which are integral to building strong and principled businesses.

Setting realistic boundaries

In the quest for success, setting boundaries is a vital strategy that equips individuals to manage ambition while safeguarding personal well-being. Understanding the nuances of balancing work and life is crucial in this journey. Work-life balance is not just a popular phrase; it's an essential practice that requires clearly dividing professional commitments from personal life. By doing so, individuals can replenish their energy and improve relationships, which ultimately aids in steering clear of burnout and fostering long-term productivity.

Emphasizing the merit of saying no is another fundamental aspect of boundary-setting. The propensity to overcommit is a common pitfall in the pursuit of ambitious goals. Learning to say no to non-essential tasks is a powerful skill that preserves energy for priority projects. This discipline maintains focus on what truly matters, allowing professionals to allocate resources effectively and achieve strategic objectives without succumbing to exhaustion.

Effective communication of boundaries plays a critical role in maintaining harmony within both personal and professional environments. When individuals articulate their limits with clarity, it fosters respect and understanding among colleagues, peers, and family members. This open dialogue cultivates healthier working relationships and prevents misunderstandings, ensuring that everyone involved can operate efficiently within agreed parameters.

The dynamic nature of life necessitates regular reassessment of boundaries. As circumstances evolve, so must the limits we establish. By regularly reevaluating and adjusting these boundaries, individuals can adapt to changes while continuing to grow, ensuring that personal integrity is maintained. This flexibility promotes resilience and encourages sustainable development in both career and personal spheres.

Establishing a clear demarcation between professional and personal time is pivotal in achieving a balanced lifestyle. For instance, designating specific hours for work-related activities, such as checking emails only during office hours, helps reinforce this separation. This practice not only enhances concentration on tasks but also signals to others when you are available, thereby reducing the likelihood of encroachment on your personal time.

Recognizing emotions is intertwined with boundary-setting. Understanding one's emotional responses and identifying what triggers them is crucial. This awareness allows individuals to discern when a professional boundary needs reinforcement or when a personal issue requires attention. Cultivating emotional intelligence enhances this capability, aiding in navigating workplace challenges with poise and composure.

Honesty is another cornerstone of setting effective boundaries. Being transparent with others about the rationale behind your boundaries can foster better comprehension and respect. It enables colleagues and supervisors to accommodate your needs more effectively, thus maintaining a balanced professional atmosphere. This openness can also prompt supportive discussions with superiors who might provide guidance or resources essential for managing your workload and ambitions.

Maintaining a structured environment at home is equally important. Setting and following boundaries outside of work is as crucial as those within the workplace. For example, choosing not to engage in work-related activities during weekends or after certain hours instills a routine that nurtures relaxation and personal pursuits. For those working from home, dedicating a specific area solely to work can mitigate the risk of distractions and ensure focus during designated working hours.

Occasionally, one may face challenges in asserting boundaries, particularly if there is resistance from others. Preparing for potential confrontations by identifying what aspects you can compromise on and practicing patience is beneficial. Clear explanations of your limits and preferred alternatives can resolve misunderstandings amicably. In instances where boundaries continue to be tested, involving a supervisor or human resources can provide additional support and documentation, helping manage any future conflicts effectively.

Bringing It All Together

Balancing ambition with well-being is key to achieving sustainable success. Throughout this chapter, we've explored how recognizing and managing burnout symptoms can prevent the detrimental effects they have on both personal and professional lives. Physical, emotional, cognitive, and behavioral signs of burnout serve as indicators that it's time to reassess priorities and integrate healthier habits. By prioritizing self-care and establishing a supportive environment, individuals and organizations can foster resilience and create a nurturing atmosphere where everyone thrives without compromising mental and physical health.

Setting realistic boundaries further supports this balance by ensuring that work commitments do not overshadow personal well-being. Understanding the importance of boundaries in both personal and professional contexts helps maintain energy levels and nurture relationships. Through effective communication and flexibility, one can adapt to life's changing demands while preserving integrity and promoting growth. As they embrace this approach to balancing ambitions, they lay the groundwork for fulfilling careers and meaningful contributions within their spheres of influence.

Chapter 16

Strategic Networking for Growth

Your network is your net worth, and by connecting people with ideas and opportunities, you create a feast of growth that the richest in the world know is essential—after all, it's far more fun to share the table than to eat alone! **- The Author**

Imagine yourself hosting a potluck; everyone brings their unique dish, and while you might start with a few empty plates, by the end of the night, you've got a feast of connections, ideas, and maybe even a few new friends—just don't forget to offer dessert!

Strategic networking involves intentional efforts to cultivate connections that foster both personal and professional growth. In today's fast-paced world, where change is the only constant, it becomes imperative for individuals at all stages of their careers to focus on building networks strategically. For young professionals stepping into the workforce, strategic networking can significantly influence their career trajectories by providing insights and opportunities otherwise inaccessible. It plays a vital role in overcoming the daunting barriers of entry into competitive industries. For those mid-career, seeking new challenges or experiencing stagnation, re-engaging with strategic networks can reinvigorate their path and reignite passion, thereby opening doors to transformative experiences and professional advancements. Entrepreneurs and aspiring leaders stand to benefit immensely from these networks, as they navigate the complex landscapes of business development and leadership growth. By establishing strong, ethical connections, they can build businesses rooted in principled practices and effective collaboration.

This chapter delves into the intricate process of identifying and leveraging valuable networking opportunities. We will explore various platforms and settings, such as professional associations, social media channels, and informal gatherings, to identify which avenues align best with their career aspirations. The narrative offers practical approaches to evaluating these networks to ensure they are not just expanding their contacts but doing so meaningfully. Furthermore, the chapter emphasizes the importance of maintaining quality relationships over sheer quantity, ensuring each connection is purposeful and mutually beneficial. Techniques for approaching influential figures within one's desired field are detailed, offering advice on how to use existing networks to facilitate introductions and create lasting professional relationships. Through preparation, active participation, and consistent follow-up, individuals are guided on how to effectively engage in industry events to maximize their exposure and solidify new relationships. In understanding how to prioritize meaningful connections, this chapter provides individuals with the knowledge and tools to strategically network for sustained growth and success in their respective fields.

Identifying Valuable Networking Opportunities

Navigating the vast landscape of networking opportunities can be challenging yet immensely rewarding. For those eager to unlock personal and professional growth, understanding how to identify and exploit these prospects is crucial. The key lies in evaluating various networking platforms and leveraging them strategically to meet specific career goals.

Different networking arenas like professional associations, social media, and informal gatherings each offer unique advantages. Professional associations serve as fertile grounds for cultivating relationships within your industry. They provide a structured environment where you can connect with peers, participate in specialized workshops, and take advantage of mentorship programs. Associations often host events allowing members to engage directly with industry leaders, gaining insights that can propel one's career forward. For instance, joining an association related to your field not only builds technical competency but also expands your awareness of emerging trends, equipping you with knowledge that can give you an edge over competitors.

Social media, particularly platforms like LinkedIn, are indispensable tools for networking. They allow for constant interaction without geographical barriers, enabling users to maintain connections with professionals worldwide. The ability to join relevant groups and participate in discussions enhances visibility and keeps you updated on industry developments. Additionally, online networks facilitate introductions through mutual connections, which can lead to rapport-building with influential figures. However, it's essential to approach social media with clarity about your objectives, ensuring that every connection and interaction furthers your professional ambitions.

Informal gatherings, such as community events or casual meetups, present opportunities to forge authentic relationships in more relaxed settings. These venues allow you to showcase your personality outside the confines of your professional role, creating bonds that might translate into business opportunities later. Engaging in volunteer work at these events can also highlight your leadership skills and commitment, attributes that often attract positive attention from potential collaborators or employers.

When targeting individuals who could be influential, research is instrumental. Begin by identifying key players within your desired field or organization. Use available resources like company websites, social media profiles, and industry publications to gather background information. Once you have identified potential contacts, approach them strategically by emphasizing shared connections or common interests. This approach can lend credibility to your outreach efforts, making it more likely that they will respond positively. Moreover, leveraging existing networks, such as colleagues or mentors, to facilitate introductions can significantly enhance your chances of building valuable connections.

Participating effectively in industry events and workshops requires careful preparation and active follow-up. Before attending, familiarize yourself with the agenda, speakers, and attendees. Having this knowledge enables you to plan targeted interactions, ensuring you maximize your time and exposure. Prepare a concise introduction about yourself, highlighting your current role and aspirations, to leave a memorable impression. At the event, engage in meaningful conversations, listen actively, and exchange contact details with new acquaintances.

Subsequently, following up is crucial to solidify these new relationships. A well-crafted email expressing gratitude and referencing specific points discussed during your meeting can reinforce the connection. Aim to maintain regular contact, perhaps by sending articles of mutual interest or sharing updates on your progress. This continued interaction not only demonstrates your commitment but keeps you top-of-mind when opportunities arise.

While connecting with numerous individuals may seem advantageous, prioritizing quality over quantity in networking is paramount. Building fewer, but deeper connections ensures that interactions are meaningful and mutually beneficial. Such relationships are more likely to yield lasting opportunities, as genuine rapport fosters trust and collaboration. Focusing on establishing a few strong ties rather than many superficial ones also allows for more substantial exchanges of ideas and support, ultimately contributing to more significant growth.

Cultivating Authentic Relationships

In an ever-evolving professional landscape, forming genuine relationships anchored in trust and collaboration is crucial for personal and career advancement. Building strong networks begins with establishing trust through transparency. Transparency means being open and honest about your intentions and actions. It involves sharing necessary information willingly and not withholding details that could impact others' decisions. Transparency also requires accountability—owning up to mistakes and working toward solutions together. Trust grows when individuals feel assured that communication will be sincere and straightforward, fostering a reliable environment conducive to collaboration.

Effective communication forms the backbone of strategic networking. For young professionals entering the workforce or mid-career individuals seeking growth, mastering active listening is vital in nurturing these connections. Active listening goes beyond hearing words; it involves comprehensively engaging with the speaker. This includes maintaining eye contact, nodding at pertinent moments, and providing verbal acknowledgments such as "I understand" or "That's interesting." These small gestures show respect for the speaker's thoughts, encouraging them to share more openly. Listening attentively without distractions like phones or side conversations helps build rapport by demonstrating genuine interest in the other person's perspective.

In addition to verbal cues, nonverbal communication plays a significant role in active listening. Body language, like leaning in slightly or using facial expressions that match the conversation's tone, can communicate empathy and involvement. Equally important is paraphrasing or summarizing points to confirm understanding, which signals that you are genuinely processing the information shared. Asking open-ended questions also enriches conversations by inviting expansive responses, thereby deepening the dialogue and creating opportunities for further engagement.

Finding mutual interests with potential partners or colleagues can significantly strengthen and cement relationships. Shared hobbies, passions, or professional interests create a common ground that facilitates discussions outside professional contexts. For instance, two professionals passionate about environmental sustainability might collaborate on a project aimed at reducing workplace waste. Such collaborations not only benefit the immediate tasks but also reinforce personal bonds through shared achievements and mutual support. Engaging in joint ventures or attending events centered around mutual interests can lead to innovative projects and long-lasting partnerships.

Networking isn't solely about initial meetings; maintaining these connections through consistent communication is equally crucial. Regular check-ins foster familiarity and reliability. Whether it's a brief message to share industry news, a congratulatory note for an achieved milestone, or arranging occasional meetings over coffee, these interactions keep acquaintances within your network updated on your activities and vice versa. This consistency aids in transforming casual connections into trusted allies who can offer assistance and insights when needed.

Being consistent in communication also means responding promptly to messages and honoring commitments made during conversations. Reliability builds confidence, ensuring that others perceive you as dependable, which is key in fostering deeper relationships. Creating a routine for reaching out can help maintain these connections, ensuring they remain vibrant despite busy schedules. For example, setting reminders to touch base with contacts every few months can prevent relationships from waning over time.

While transparency, active listening, and shared interests lay the groundwork, nurturing a reputation for being trustworthy amplifies these efforts. Upholding promises and delivering on your word strengthens your reliability. When others know that you consistently follow through on your commitments, they become more inclined to reciprocate, thereby facilitating an atmosphere of mutual respect and collaboration. Furthermore, acknowledging and appreciating contributions from others solidifies these networks, ensuring everyone feels valued and recognized for their input.

Providing Value to Connections

In the dynamic world of professional growth, a strategic approach to networking is critical. One such strategy is fostering stronger networks through contributing to others' successes, emphasizing the concept of reciprocity. A key element is identifying opportunities to help connections and understanding the importance of giving before receiving. Much like planting seeds in a garden, your contributions can nurture the growth of relationships that flower into diverse professional opportunities.

Recognizing chances to assist others requires an observant and proactive mindset. It's about finding areas where your skills can complement someone else's goals. For instance, offering insights on a project or providing access to useful contacts not only helps others but also establishes you as a valuable partner. Think of it as investing in relationship capital, where returns are measured in mutual support and collaboration.

Guideline: To identify these opportunities effectively, start by assessing the needs and goals of those in your network. Pay attention during conversations and listen for cues where your expertise might be of use. This could involve mentoring a junior colleague, sharing industry reports with peers, or simply being a sounding board for new ideas.

Another vital aspect of strategic networking is sharing knowledge and resources. When you willingly share what you know or have access to, you position yourself as a resourceful expert. Techniques for achieving this include organizing workshops, writing insightful articles, or even creating forums for discussions.

These actions not only enhance your reputation but also establish your presence as a thought leader in your field.

Guideline: Ensure that the information or resources you share are relevant and bring genuine value. Tailor your contributions to align with the interests and needs of your network. By doing so, you make your interactions more meaningful and ensure that your efforts are appreciated and remembered.

Collaboration is equally important in building reciprocal relationships. Encouraging joint projects or efforts that yield mutual benefits creates a strong foundation for enduring networks. These win-win situations often lead to innovative outcomes that neither party could achieve alone. For instance, co-authoring a publication, developing a new product feature with a peer, or partnering on a community initiative can open doors for both parties involved.

Guideline: Approach each collaborative opportunity with an open mind and willingness to adapt. Clearly define shared goals and expectations from the outset to ensure alignment. Regular check-ins and constructive feedback foster trust and keep the collaboration on track.

While contributing to others' success, recognizing and acknowledging the contributions of your connections is pivotal. It's easy to overlook small acts of kindness or support, but expressing gratitude reinforces bonds and encourages continued support. Whether it's sending a thoughtful thank-you note or publicly praising someone's efforts, these gestures go a long way in cementing professional relationships.

Understanding that networking is not just about personal gain, but about building a community of supportive professionals, is crucial. When you focus on contributing to others, you create an environment where everyone thrives. Reciprocity becomes a natural byproduct of these interactions, forming a network that is resilient, resourceful, and ready to rise to challenges.

Final Thoughts

In this chapter, we've explored how building strategic networks can significantly enhance both personal and professional growth. By identifying valuable networking opportunities in different arenas—like professional associations, social media, and informal gatherings—you open doors to meaningful connections that can propel your career forward. We've discussed the importance of targeted engagements, such as participating in industry events and leveraging existing relationships through careful research and preparation. The key takeaway is to prioritize quality over quantity, focusing on deep, genuine connections that foster trust and mutual benefit.

Moreover, cultivating authentic relationships requires transparency and effective communication. Building trust starts with being open about intentions and consistently following through on commitments. Active listening and finding common interests with others strengthen these bonds, allowing you to support each other's goals collaboratively. Providing value to your network by sharing knowledge and resources further enhances your position as a resourceful partner. Ultimately, networking isn't just about what you gain but also about creating a supportive community where everyone thrives through shared successes and reciprocal actions.

Chapter 17

Continuous Learning and Self-Improvement

The only limits to our future are the doubts we carry today; by kindling our minds through continuous learning, we uncover the opportunities hidden in the midst of challenges. **- The Author**

Imagine yourself trying to assemble a piece of IKEA furniture; you might face confusion and a few extra screws, but each instruction learned, and the mistake made brings you one step closer to creating something surprisingly sturdy and beautiful—just remember to keep the manual handy!

Continuous learning and self-improvement play a pivotal role in personal and professional development, especially in an ever-evolving world. The commitment to these lifelong pursuits ensures that individuals remain adaptable, resilient, and prepared for the challenges that accompany change. In our rapidly shifting environments, those who prioritize consistent growth can navigate their careers with confidence and maintain a competitive edge. By embracing a mindset centered around continuous learning, individuals unlock opportunities that foster both personal fulfillment and professional success, paving the way for transformative experiences that shape future possibilities.

This chapter delves into key strategies and methods that empower readers on their journey of ongoing improvement. It begins by exploring how to identify personal areas for development through introspection and the adaptation of techniques such as SWOT analysis. These tools offer structured guidance in evaluating one's strengths and weaknesses while recognizing opportunities and threats in various contexts. The subsequent discussion highlights the significance of prioritizing skills that align with career aspirations, ensuring that self-improvement efforts are directed towards meaningful objectives. Setting specific benchmarks plays a crucial role in tracking progress, and facilitating a systematic approach to personal enhancement. Furthermore, the chapter underscores the importance of seeking regular feedback, thereby fostering a culture of accountability and engagement. By incorporating these elements, we can construct an ecosystem of growth, equipped with the resources needed to excel in competitive landscapes. Through this comprehensive exploration, individuals are encouraged to embrace the concept of continuous learning as an integral part of their professional lives, ultimately driving them toward greater achievements and adaptability.

Identifying Areas for Development

Understanding where you stand in terms of skills and areas for improvement is fundamental to personal growth and self-improvement. The first step towards achieving this involves a thorough self-reflection process. This introspective practice allows individuals to gain insight into their strengths and weaknesses, facilitating targeted development efforts that lead to continuous improvement.

One effective approach to enhancing self-awareness and identifying areas for growth is through the use of strategic tools such as SWOT analysis. Originally designed for business environments, SWOT—standing for Strengths, Weaknesses, Opportunities, and Threats—offers a structured framework that can be adapted for personal reflection. By evaluating your internal strengths and weaknesses alongside external opportunities and threats, you develop a comprehensive picture of your current state and future potential. Engaging with others during this analysis, whether friends, family, or professional mentors, can provide diverse perspectives that enrich your understanding and highlight blind spots that may have been overlooked. This collaboration not only enriches the analysis but also fosters a support network that can motivate you on your journey of self-improvement.

Moreover, prioritizing which skills to focus on is crucial for aligning personal development with career advancement and personal fulfillment. It's important to concentrate on capabilities that will make the most significant impact on your professional journey. For instance, young professionals entering the workforce might prioritize improving communication skills, which are essential for effective teamwork and leadership roles. Similarly, mid-career individuals looking to break free from stagnation could benefit from enhancing emotional intelligence to better manage interpersonal relationships and increase workplace influence. Entrepreneurs and aspiring leaders should consider focusing on skills that strengthen ethical practices and team empowerment, contributing to a positive organizational culture.

To maintain progress in these targeted areas, setting specific benchmarks is essential. These benchmarks act as measurable goals that help track improvements and ensure a structured approach to self-development. Clear milestones enable individuals to evaluate their progress over time, allowing for adjustments and recalibration of strategies as needed. For example, if one of your goals is to improve public speaking skills, you might start by setting a benchmark to deliver a presentation at a small team meeting. Gradually, you could aim for larger audiences or more complex topics, utilizing each milestone to build confidence and refine techniques.

Regular feedback is another vital component of the self-improvement journey. Seeking opinions and insights from peers, mentors, or colleagues facilitates an interactive learning environment. Feedback provides clarity on how others perceive your progress and areas needing further attention. Constructive criticism serves as a reality check and guides you toward more effective strategies for overcoming challenges. Establishing a routine for receiving and reflecting on feedback promotes accountability and ensures ongoing engagement with your personal development goals.

Incorporating these practices into your routine demands discipline and commitment. Self-assessment using tools like SWOT analysis establishes a foundation for understanding oneself better, while prioritizing skills aligns developmental activities with career aspirations. Setting benchmarks offers metrics to gauge advancement, and consistent feedback engages community insights, creating an ecosystem of growth and accountability.

Utilizing Diverse Learning Resources

In today's fast-paced world, continuous learning and self-improvement are vital for adaptability and success. To effectively harness the power of learning, one must explore various resources and methods available. Engaging with literature across diverse genres is a potent tool for expanding knowledge and enhancing creative thinking. Reading different types of books exposes individuals to new ideas, perspectives, and cultures, cultivating a more comprehensive understanding of the world. Fiction can spark creativity and empathy by placing the reader in the minds and lives of characters vastly different from themselves, while non-fiction provides factual insights and knowledge about specific subjects. By diversifying reading material, learners can develop a well-rounded mindset and improve their ability to think critically.

Another vital resource is online courses and webinars, which have revolutionized the way we learn. These digital platforms offer access to global expertise and facilitate professional development, allowing individuals to acquire new skills at their own pace and convenience. Whether it's mastering a new language, delving into data analytics, or exploring leadership strategies, online courses provide structured learning environments with expert guidance. It's crucial, however, to select courses that align with personal or career goals to maximize their benefit. Establishing a habit of regular learning through these mediums ensures that individuals stay current with industry trends and advancements, ultimately enhancing their employability and competency.

Networking and mentorship constitute another crucial element in leveraging resources for effective learning. Through networking, individuals can connect with like-minded professionals, share experiences, and exchange valuable insights. This exchange fosters a deeper understanding of industry practices and challenges, enabling learners to gain diverse perspectives. Mentorship, on the other hand, offers personalized guidance and support. By learning from others' experiences, mentees can avoid common pitfalls and accelerate their growth. A mentor can provide invaluable advice, helping mentees navigate complex situations and make informed decisions. Building strong relationships through networking and mentorship not only aids in skill development but also strengthens community connections and collaboration.

Experiential learning is a powerful method for applying theoretical knowledge practically, ultimately enhancing one's understanding and retention of information. Participating in internships or real-world projects allows learners to immerse themselves in authentic work environments where they can apply concepts learned in a classroom setting. For example, an engineering student might intern at a tech company, applying their technical learning to solve real-world problems. This direct application of knowledge not only solidifies understanding but also builds confidence in one's abilities. Moreover, experiential learning helps learners adapt to workplace dynamics and hone interpersonal skills such as communication, teamwork, and problem-solving, which are essential for career advancement.

When engaging in online courses and webinars, it's important to establish clear goals and remain committed to completing the chosen program. One guideline for maximizing the benefits of online learning is to actively participate in discussions and forums associated with the course. Engaging with fellow learners helps reinforce knowledge and clarifies doubts. Another key strategy is to set aside dedicated time each week to focus on the coursework, treating it as seriously as any in-person class. Maintaining consistency and discipline ensures continuity in learning and helps in achieving desired outcomes. Additionally, reflecting on what has been learned and how it applies to one's career or personal development can enhance the overall learning experience.

When utilizing networking and mentorship opportunities, aim to be proactive and open to new experiences. Start by identifying potential mentors or networks that align with your interests or career goals. Attend conferences, join professional associations, and engage in online communities to broaden your reach. Remember, meaningful connections require effort: reach out to individuals, ask questions, and express genuine interest in their work. When seeking a mentor, look for someone whose career path inspires you and whose values resonate with your own. Once a mentoring relationship is established, maintain regular communication, clearly articulate your learning objectives, and be receptive to feedback. Practicing gratitude and acknowledging the mentor's influence encourages a supportive and productive relationship.

Finally, when participating in experiential learning, approach each opportunity with an open mind and readiness to embrace new challenges. Seek internships or projects that cater to your area of interest but also push you slightly out of your comfort zone. During these experiences, focus on absorbing as much practical knowledge as possible—ask questions, volunteer for tasks, and reflect on both successes and failures. The lessons learned from real-world scenarios are often unmatched by theoretical studies alone. Keep a journal to document experiences, insights, and areas for improvement, allowing you to track progress and identify patterns over time. This reflective practice enhances self-awareness and guides future learning endeavors.

Setting Specific Educational Goals

Setting clear, defined goals is a fundamental element in the continuous learning journey. These goals serve as the compass that guides learners through educational pursuits, providing motivation and a sense of direction. Without them, efforts may become unfocused, and progress can stagnate. One effective way to establish clarity and purpose in learning is by utilizing the SMART Goals Framework, which stands for Specific, Measurable, Achievable, Relevant, and Time-bound.

The SMART Goals Framework is a powerful tool that helps define precise objectives, making it easier to channel efforts effectively. A specific goal eliminates ambiguity. For example, rather than aiming to "learn more about marketing," a more targeted goal would be to "complete an online course on digital marketing strategies within three months." This specificity makes it clearer what steps need to be taken and allows for a focused approach to learning. Making goals measurable further ensures that one can track progress and make necessary adjustments along the way. Measuring outcomes such as completing certain modules or obtaining a certification offers tangible evidence of advancement. An achievable goal ensures that aspirations are realistic and attainable with available resources and time, preventing discouragement from overly ambitious targets. It's also vital that goals remain relevant to broader personal or professional ambitions, aligning with where one wants to see growth or change. Lastly, having a time-bound element introduces a deadline, creating urgency and encouraging consistency in pursuing these educational objectives.

While the SMART framework provides structure to goal setting, understanding the distinction between long-term and short-term goals is crucial for balancing immediate actions with future aspirations. Long-term goals provide a vision or endpoint that can shape one's overall learning trajectory. These could include mastering a new language or earning a degree, which requires sustained effort over a considerable period. Short-term goals, meanwhile, are milestones on the path to achieving long-term ambitions. They might involve completing a chapter of a textbook weekly or attending a seminar related to your field of interest. This differentiation ensures that there is a balance between working towards substantial achievements while maintaining momentum with smaller, more easily conquered tasks.

In addition to using frameworks and differentiating goals, visual techniques like vision boards can help reinforce these objectives. Vision boards act as a daily visual reminder of one's goals, keeping them at the forefront of the mind and invigorating commitment. By selecting images, words, and symbols that represent important aspirations, individuals create a tactile representation of their ambitions. For instance, someone aiming to improve their public speaking skills might include pictures of inspiring speakers or venues they'd like to present in. Displaying this personalized collage in a prominent place serves as both inspiration and a constant reminder of why the effort is worthwhile.

Equally important is establishing routines for regular reflection on these goals. The dynamic nature of learning means that adaptability is often required. What was once a priority might change due to evolving interests or external circumstances.

Regularly assessing progress helps identify what is working and where adjustments are needed. Reflection could be in the form of journaling, discussing achievements and challenges with a mentor, or simply setting aside time each week to evaluate and recalibrate goals. This ongoing process not only aids in maintaining focus but also fosters a proactive attitude towards overcoming obstacles and seizing new opportunities.

Concluding Thoughts

Commitment to continuous learning is at the heart of personal and professional growth. This chapter has explored various strategies for identifying areas for improvement, emphasizing the importance of self-reflection, feedback, and the use of structured tools like SWOT analysis. These methods help individuals understand their strengths and address weaknesses by setting targeted goals aligned with their aspirations. Whether you're a young professional starting out or an experienced entrepreneur aiming to enhance your leadership skills, adopting these practices can lead to meaningful development. By engaging with mentors and embracing diverse resources, you create a support network that motivates ongoing progress.

The journey of learning is dynamic and requires adaptability to new challenges. Utilizing diverse learning tools such as online courses, literature, and experiential opportunities enables individuals to acquire new skills and insights effectively. Networking and mentorship further enrich this process, providing guidance and fostering community connections. Setting specific goals, whether they are short-term milestones or long-term aspirations, provides direction and maintains focus in the ever-evolving landscape of personal and career development. As we move forward, the dedication to lifelong learning ensures that we remain adaptable, capable, and ready to grasp opportunities, ultimately achieving success and fulfillment in our chosen paths.

Chapter 18

Living with Integrity and Authenticity

Living with integrity means doing the right thing out of a commitment to our values, while authenticity invites us to embrace our true selves, reminding us that our greatest leadership tool is the genuine example we set for others. **- The Author**

Imagine yourself wearing your favorite pair of socks; they might not match everyone else's idea of style, but they feel comfortable and true to you, and in the end, you'll be the one dancing happily while others are busy adjusting their shoes!

Living with integrity and authenticity is a matter of aligning one's actions and decisions with personal values and ethical standards. This alignment not only shapes individual behavior but also significantly impacts one's reputation, making it a vital consideration for those fostering personal and professional growth. Integrity acts as a compass, guiding individuals through the complexities of life while ensuring their actions reflect their true beliefs and intentions. Authenticity, on the other hand, involves embracing and expressing one's genuine self without compromise. Together, they form the cornerstone of trustworthy character, providing stability and direction in an ever-evolving world. For young professionals eager to establish themselves, maintaining integrity and authenticity can be pivotal in serving as differentiators in competitive settings. Similarly, mid-career individuals seeking renewed motivation find that these principles offer clarity and resilience amidst career transitions. Entrepreneurs and aspiring leaders recognize them as essential traits for cultivating ethical businesses and inspiring others.

Within this chapter, you are invited to explore the intricacies of personal ethics and values as they relate to integrity and authenticity. The discussion begins by examining how defining these core principles can influence decision-making processes, enhancing both personal and professional reputations. Through introspection and reflection, individuals learn to identify what truly matters to them, enabling authentic living and minimizing internal conflict. The chapter delves into practical strategies for crafting personal codes of ethics, offering guidance on aligning actions with deeply held beliefs. By tackling real-world scenarios and challenges, you gain insights into applying these concepts effectively, reinforcing integrity amidst adversity. Additionally, the importance of transparency and consistency in building trust is highlighted, illustrating how clear communication and reliable commitments enhance relationships and leadership. Ultimately, this exploration empowers individuals, whether just starting their careers or leading organizations, to navigate their journeys with confidence and moral fortitude, creating environments where they and others can thrive authentically.

Understanding Personal Ethics and Values

Establishing personal ethics and values is crucial for anyone seeking to live with integrity and authenticity, which form the foundation of a trustworthy reputation. By defining and living by these principles, individuals not only guide their behavior but also carve out identities that align with deeply held beliefs. Understanding personal ethics involves delving into the core principles that steer both actions and decisions. These principles shape how we interact with the world and are vital in establishing reputations. When we comprehend what drives our choices, it becomes easier to navigate life's complexities with confidence and consistency.

Defining one's personal ethics requires introspection. This process involves identifying what you stand for and aligning your actions with these beliefs. It might seem challenging to pinpoint your ethical standpoint, especially when modern life presents numerous conflicting demands and expectations. However, clear personal ethics serve as an internal compass, offering direction and stability amidst chaos. By understanding these guiding principles, individuals can make decisions that reflect their true selves, fostering authenticity and strengthening their professional and personal reputations.

Identifying core values is equally critical. Core values act as benchmarks for decision-making and emotional well-being, highlighting priorities and ensuring actions resonate with genuine intentions. Clarity about these values enables individuals to prioritize effectively, leading to more authentic and fulfilling lives. When you understand your core values, you can establish goals and pursuits that align with what truly matters to you, reducing internal conflict and enhancing emotional satisfaction.

To identify these core values, a guideline may involve listing key aspects of life that hold significant importance. Reflect on past experiences, considering what brought satisfaction or discomfort. Ask questions like, "What do I admire most in others?" and "What behaviors make me proud of myself?" Such reflections offer insights into previously unexamined motivations. Engaging in this process helps clarify personal priorities, allowing individuals to craft lives that genuinely reflect their deepest aspirations and contribute positively to their sense of self.

The impact of values on decision-making cannot be overstated. Values serve as the backdrop against which choices are made, influencing how we approach opportunities and challenges. Decisions aligned with core values foster accountability to oneself and others. They provide a framework within which individuals can evaluate options, ensuring that actions taken are consistent with their ideals and principles. This alignment is crucial for personal integrity; it reinforces a sense of responsibility and enhances trustworthiness among peers.

Moreover, values-based decision-making often results in fewer regrets and more satisfying outcomes. When choices align with values, individuals are more likely to feel contentment and less inner conflict. For example, someone who values honesty will find greater long-term peace and satisfaction in a career that promotes transparency over one that requires compromising those ideals. Consistent reflection ensures that values remain at the heart of every decision, thereby upholding accountability and maintaining the integrity of one's character.

Personal reflection strategies play an important role in developing self-awareness and resilience amidst evolving circumstances. Regular contemplation of personal ethics and values fosters a deeper understanding of oneself. Such ongoing reflection encourages growth and adaptability, qualities increasingly necessary in today's fast-paced world. Strategies for reflection include journaling, meditation, or engaging in discussions that challenge and refine your perceptions. These practices help cultivate greater self-awareness, enabling individuals to recognize areas where they thrive and those requiring further development.

A practical guideline here could be setting aside regular intervals for reflection—perhaps weekly or monthly sessions dedicated to evaluating one's actions and thoughts against personal values. During this time, consider whether recent decisions were congruent with your principles and identify any misalignments. This exercise aids in adjusting behavior, ensuring continued alignment with core values. Over time, this habit strengthens resilience, equipping individuals to face adversity while remaining true to their convictions.

Besides benefiting personal growth, such practices can enhance interpersonal relationships and professional accomplishments. Individuals who regularly reflect on their values are better equipped to communicate authentically, thus improving mutual understanding and respect in relationships. In professional settings, this clarity translates to consistent, principled leadership, inspiring others through actions rather than just words.

Making Decisions Aligned with Integrity

In the journey of personal and professional development, one of the most defining traits is living with integrity and authenticity. Making decisions that genuinely reflect one's values not only bolsters self-esteem but also cultivates a reliable reputation. This process begins with structured decision-making frameworks, which are invaluable when faced with complex situations. Such frameworks can guide individuals to make principled choices by evaluating all facets of a challenge, considering possible outcomes, and prioritizing core values. By doing so, young professionals, mid-career individuals, and aspiring leaders can foster confidence in their abilities to navigate ethical dilemmas.

When individuals evaluate their choices against established values, they pave the way for authentic decisions. This reflection aligns actions with beliefs, resulting in greater self-trust and integrity. For instance, a young professional entering the workforce might face a situation where accepting a bribe could expedite project completion. However, by assessing this choice against personal and organizational values of honesty and transparency, the individual can opt to refuse the bribe, thereby reinforcing a trustworthy image and upholding moral principles. This evaluative process ensures that actions taken resonate with inner convictions and reinforce one's character.

Understanding the consequences of decisions further highlights the importance of responsible thinking. Each choice impacts relationships, work dynamics, and personal integrity, making it crucial to weigh both immediate effects and long-term repercussions. For example, a manager deciding whether to delegate tasks to inexperienced team members should consider how this might influence team morale and performance. While delegating can promote growth and skill development, it's essential to ensure that support structures are in place to mitigate potential negative outcomes. In such scenarios, being mindful of consequences not only strengthens decision-making but also aids in fostering effective relationship management.

Equally important is a commitment to ethical standards, which play a pivotal role in promoting respect and trust. When facing adversity or unforeseen challenges, adhering to ethical principles elevates leadership and character. Consider an entrepreneur managing a startup during economic uncertainty—by committing to fair labor practices and honest communication with stakeholders, they set a foundation of integrity that attracts respect from employees and investors alike. Upholding ethical standards, even when inconvenient or challenging, sends a powerful message about one's commitment to trustworthiness and moral fortitude.

Implementing these concepts requires a practical approach. A structured decision-making framework would typically involve identifying ethical issues, gathering relevant facts, evaluating alternatives, choosing an option for action, and reflecting on outcomes. Such a framework helps maintain objectivity and clarity in decision-making processes. By considering various perspectives and seeking diverse opinions before finalizing decisions, individuals can ensure that their actions align with both personal beliefs and community standards.

Furthermore, cultivating a personal code of ethics serves as a compass guiding through complexities. This reflective exercise allows individuals to understand what truly matters and how they wish to conduct themselves in diverse situations. Entrepreneurs, for example, may develop codes emphasizing sustainability, customer service excellence, and employee welfare. These guidelines not only support ethical decision-making but also enhance consistency across actions, thus promoting a unified vision throughout the organization.

Being Transparent and Consistent

Transparency and consistency are crucial elements in building trust and integrity. They serve as the foundation upon which reliable relationships are constructed, influencing both personal and professional interactions.

Transparency in communication sets the stage for trust by fostering open dialogue and understanding. When individuals communicate openly, they create opportunities to connect at a deeper level, reducing the likelihood of misunderstandings. For example, a manager who is transparent about company goals and challenges encourages team members to engage more effectively, knowing they have complete information. Such openness not only builds trust but also strengthens resilience within teams, as members feel empowered to share their thoughts and ideas without fear of reprisal. This environment encourages collaboration and innovation, vital for any organization or relationship seeking growth and success.

Consistency in aligning behavior with commitments further enhances the perception of reliability and trustworthiness. When individuals consistently act in accordance with their commitments, they project a cohesive identity that others can depend on. Consider the case of a business leader who always delivers on promises and aligns actions with stated values. This leader establishes a reputation for integrity, cementing trust with employees, clients, and stakeholders alike. Consistent actions reassure others that principles dictate decision-making processes, leading to stable and predictable outcomes. This predictability allows people to form enduring bonds rooted in shared understanding and mutual respect.

Creating trust through reliability involves regularly honoring commitments, a practice that bolsters both personal and professional relationships. Whether it's meeting deadlines, attending important events, or simply being present when needed, fulfilling promises demonstrates an unwavering sense of responsibility. In professional environments, this might involve consistently delivering quality work, thereby earning the confidence of colleagues and supervisors. In personal relationships, reliability manifests as being a dependable friend or partner, someone others can count on during times of need. By building a track record of dependability, trust naturally follows, enriching all forms of interaction.

To maintain consistency, one must employ strategies that ensure alignment between actions and beliefs. Mindfulness is an effective approach, encouraging individuals to remain conscious of their intentions and actions. By staying aware of how one's behavior reflects personal values, mindfulness helps in maintaining consistency even amidst changing circumstances. Feedback loops provide another critical mechanism for ensuring alignment. Regularly seeking feedback from peers or mentors offers valuable insights into areas where alignment may falter. Acting on this feedback enables course correction, refining actions to better match intended values. These strategies promote an ongoing evaluation of actions, reinforcing the integrity of commitments made.

A real-world example of transparency and consistency can be seen in successful brand management. Brands that clearly communicate their values and practices while maintaining a consistent message across all touchpoints tend to cultivate strong consumer loyalty. Authenticity and consistency are key pillars in the trust-building process, allowing brands to resonate deeply with their audience over time. Consumers who perceive brands as genuine and sincere are likely to remain engaged, advocating for them and contributing to long-lasting relationships.

Similarly, in leadership, transparency equates to openly sharing the reasoning behind decisions and acknowledging both successes and failures. From my experience in Excellence, Communication and Leadership (since 1990), I have witnessed that, leaders who prioritize transparency gain respect and trust from their teams. This openness creates a ripple effect, encouraging others within the organization to adopt similar practices, thus embedding a culture of honesty and integrity.

Incorporating these principles into personal development entails cultivating habits that reflect both transparency and consistency. Individuals aspiring to grow in their careers or enhance their leadership abilities can benefit from adopting straightforward and truthful communication styles while ensuring their actions consistently reflect their values and commitments. Moreover, by regularly evaluating their behavior and seeking constructive feedback, they align closer to their true selves, enhancing authenticity and trust in their interactions.

In conclusion, transparency and consistency are not merely desirable traits but essential components of trustworthy and integrative relationships. Through transparent communication and consistent alignment of actions with commitments, individuals and organizations can build solid foundations of trust, resulting in more meaningful connections and sustainable success. Integrating mindfulness and feedback into daily routines ensures that principles remain aligned with actions, supporting continued growth in personal and professional capacities.

Reflection

Living authentically and with integrity is the cornerstone of building a trustworthy reputation. This chapter has delved into the importance of personal ethics and values, guiding individuals to explore and define what truly matters to them. By understanding and aligning actions with core principles, one can navigate life's complexities with confidence and create a consistent identity that earns respect. The discussions have shown how personal introspection, and the establishment of clear ethical standards act as an internal compass, aiding in decision-making and enhancing both professional and personal relationships. Regular reflection on these values not only strengthens self-awareness but also fuels resilience in dynamic environments.

Decisions rooted in personal ethics foster authenticity and strengthen reputations. By evaluating choices against established values, individuals can make principled decisions that resonate with their beliefs. This reflective process supports consistency between one's actions and commitments, which is essential for maintaining trust. Moreover, transparency plays a crucial role in building dependable relationships, whether through straightforward communication or reliable behavior. Implementing strategies such as regular feedback and mindfulness ensures ongoing alignment between actions and principles. As illustrated in this chapter, living with integrity and transparency leads to meaningful connections and sustainable success, encouraging growth across various facets of life and work.

Chapter 19

Leveraging Technology for Productivity

Leveraging technology turns the engine of change into a powerful tool that brings people together, helping us focus not on doing more, but on doing what truly matters most. **- The Author**

Imagine yourself having a Swiss Army knife; with the right tool at your fingertips, you can slice through challenges, open up new opportunities, and navigate complexities—just be sure you know which tool to use, or you might end up with a corkscrew when all you needed was a screwdriver!

Leveraging technology for productivity has become an essential pursuit in our contemporary, fast-paced world. As individuals strive to enhance efficiency and streamline their workflows, the selection and effective application of technological tools play a pivotal role in achieving these goals. This chapter delves into the process of leveraging technology by guiding you through identifying tools that align perfectly with your unique work style. It begins with exploring how personal workflows can be assessed to pinpoint areas where technology might streamline processes, optimize routines, and tackle inefficiencies. By understanding your current practices, you can uncover opportunities for automation or efficient management of tasks, ultimately setting the foundation for increased productivity.

The chapter then shifts focus towards exploring a variety of productivity tools available in today's market. This exploration emphasizes informed decision-making and collaboration, encouraging individuals to sample various tools tailored to their needs—be it task management, document collaboration, or communication applications. Approaching these tools with a trial-and-error mindset is encouraged, as experimentation allows discovering which solutions best complement individual habits and improve productivity. The narrative also provides insights into valuable recommendations and reviews that can aid in selecting efficient and highly rated tools. Moreover, by harnessing community suggestions and expert opinions, you are better equipped to make choices that yield significant boosts in efficiency and foster positive transformations in work processes. Throughout this journey, the emphasis is placed on finding the right technological fit to enhance not only individual productivity but also overall teamwork and collaborative dynamics within professional settings.

Identifying tools that suit individual needs

In today's fast-paced world, leveraging technology for productivity is crucial for achieving success in both personal and professional spheres. The abundance of available tools offers exciting opportunities to enhance efficiency, streamline workflows, and optimize work styles. However, with so many options, it can be challenging to find the right fit. To address this, it's essential to guide you on identifying technology tools that align with your unique work styles.

To begin, assessing personal workflows is a key step in uncovering areas where technology can streamline processes. Everyone has distinct routines and preferences for managing tasks. By taking a closer look at how you currently handle your daily activities, you can identify inefficiencies or repetitive tasks that could benefit from automation or more efficient management. For instance, if you spend too much time organizing emails, perhaps an email management tool like SaneBox could help by prioritizing messages and decluttering your inbox. Similarly, if scheduling meetings is a hassle, consider an AI-powered scheduling tool such as Motion, which integrates seamlessly with personal and work calendars to auto-schedule based on priorities and deadlines.

Once you've identified areas for improvement, exploring various productivity tools is crucial. This exploration provides opportunities for informed decision-making and collaboration, enabling you to select tools tailored to your needs. With numerous apps available, take the time to research different categories of tools—such as task management, document collaboration, and communication apps— to understand their functionalities. For example, Notion is known for its central hub for information storage with AI integration, making it ideal for team collaboration and project organization. By sampling different tools, you not only gain insights into their capabilities but also learn how they can potentially transform your work style.

Next, adopting a trial-and-error approach is an effective way to find the tools that best align with your habits and improve productivity. Not all tools will be perfect matches initially, and experimentation allows you to test which ones complement your workflow. Start with free trials or free versions of apps when possible. Use these periods to fully immerse yourself and determine whether the tool's features add value to your day-to-day tasks. Take, for example, a marketing professional trying out Midjourney or Canva to create visually appealing content. You might discover that one tool has a user interface better suited to your creative process, enhancing your productivity and reducing the time spent on design projects.

While experimenting, seeking recommendations and reviews can aid immensely in choosing efficient, highly rated tools. Hearing about others' experiences can save valuable time and guide you toward proven solutions. Platforms such as PCMag provide expert reviews of productivity apps, offering insights into their strengths and limitations. Moreover, user reviews on app stores or forums can provide real-world feedback from people in similar roles or industries, giving you a sense of how the tools perform in practice. Engaging in online communities or chatting with colleagues who have experience using various tools can further refine your choices.

Understanding the importance of selecting the right tools lies in knowing that finding a good fit can significantly boost your efficiency and lead to a positive transformation in how you work.

For young professionals just entering the workforce, adopting the right technology tools can set the foundation for a productive career. Mid-career individuals seeking growth and renewed motivation may find new energy in discovering innovative tools that revitalize stagnating routines. Entrepreneurs and aspiring leaders, aiming to build principled businesses, can empower themselves and their teams with technology, fostering a culture of productivity and collaboration.

Learning efficient digital organization techniques

In today's fast-paced world, digital organization plays a pivotal role in enhancing both personal and professional productivity. As our reliance on technology grows, so does the importance of effectively managing digital resources to maintain focus and streamline workflows. Embracing digital organization not only minimizes the time spent searching for documents but also creates a structured environment that fosters efficiency.

Utilizing folders and labeling systems is a fundamental step towards achieving digital clarity. Imagine a cluttered desktop or a chaotic set of online documents; both can make locating important files a daunting task. Implementing a consistent folder structure and clear labeling system can mitigate these issues. For instance, establishing a hierarchy where projects are divided into folders by subject or client can greatly simplify file retrieval. Labels play an equally crucial role, helping distinguish between various document types, such as drafts, final versions, or reference materials. This organizational strategy reduces frustration and saves precious time otherwise wasted in futile searches. According to research, nearly two-thirds of employees have had to recreate lost documents due to poor digital organization (Adobe Acrobat Team, 2023).

Equally important is implementing robust task management systems. As responsibilities pile up, it's easy to feel overwhelmed. Task management tools like Trello, Asana, or Monday.com allow users to prioritize tasks and visualize upcoming deadlines. By organizing tasks according to urgency and importance, individuals can efficiently navigate through their workload without feeling burdened. These tools often feature collaborative functions, making them ideal for teams working together. With a shared task board, team members can update ongoing projects and communicate seamlessly, ensuring everyone is aligned with project goals. Proper task management not only enhances individual productivity but also improves overall team performance.

Creating a focused workspace is essential to reducing distractions and boosting creativity. In a digital context, this means decluttering your virtual environment. Close unnecessary browser tabs and applications that do not contribute to the task at hand. Consider tools like website blockers to prevent access to distracting sites during work hours. A vital aspect of a focused workspace is customizing your digital interface to suit your preferences. Personal touches, such as wallpaper choices or tool placements, can make the workspace more inviting and conducive to concentration. Moreover, maintaining a clean and organized physical desk complements digital efforts, reinforcing a commitment to focus and task completion.

Setting up recurring reminders plays a crucial role in ensuring the timely completion of tasks and fostering accountability. Digital calendars and reminder apps provide automated alerts that help keep you on track without constant manual intervention. Regular notifications about approaching deadlines or scheduled meetings serve as subtle nudges, allowing you to allocate sufficient time for preparation. Additionally, recurring reminders for repeated tasks or periodic reviews establish consistency, which is especially beneficial for long-term projects. Maintaining regular intervals for certain activities helps create habits that enhance productivity over time.

To address challenges related to digital disorganization, performing regular digital cleanups can prove beneficial. Many employees report conducting digital cleanups when faced with storage limitations or system performance issues (Adobe Acrobat Team, 2023). However, making cleanups a routine practice prevents the accumulation of outdated or irrelevant data. By systematically reviewing and organizing digital assets, professionals can improve information accessibility and reduce inefficiencies caused by disorderly systems.

Integrating these practices within an organization's culture further amplifies their positive effects. Supplemental training sessions on digital organization techniques ensure all team members are equipped with the knowledge to utilize available tools effectively. Understanding folder structures, version control, and access controls can significantly enhance workflow dynamics. Providing employees with access to online courses or webinars about emerging digital tools keeps everyone current with evolving trends and capabilities.

Staying updated with new technological trends

In today's fast-paced world, staying ahead in the realm of technology can greatly boost productivity, both personally and professionally. To thrive, it's essential to be aware of emerging technologies that offer new capabilities and efficiencies. One effective strategy is following industry leaders and influencers who are at the forefront of technological advancements. These individuals often have insider knowledge about the latest tools and strategies that can optimize work processes. Social media platforms like LinkedIn and X can be valuable resources for keeping up with these thought leaders. Regularly reading their posts or subscribing to newsletters can provide insights into how they leverage technology to improve productivity.

For those eager to expand their knowledge and skills, participating in online courses and webinars is another productive approach. The digital landscape is constantly evolving, making it necessary to engage in continuous learning to remain relevant. Online platforms offer a variety of courses on emerging technologies such as artificial intelligence, blockchain, or the Internet of Things. These learning opportunities not only enhance technical skills but also promote adaptability in an ever-changing environment. A guideline here is to allocate a specific time each week dedicated to learning, ensuring that it becomes a routine part of personal development.

Experimenting trial versions of new software can also play a crucial role in enhancing productivity. Software developers often offer limited-time trials that allow users to explore their products without financial commitment. This presents an opportunity to assess various tools and determine which best aligns with one's needs. For instance, trying out different project management software can help identify which features streamline workflows most effectively. When experimenting, it's advisable to set clear objectives for what you hope to achieve with the software, whether it's improving task management or increasing collaborative efficiency.

Finally, joining professional groups and forums offers a platform for networking and collaborative innovation. Engaging with peers in your field can lead to valuable exchanges of ideas and experiences related to the use of technology in your industry. Professional organizations often host events, discussions, and workshops where members can learn from one another and gain new perspectives on leveraging technology for productivity. Through active participation, individuals can build relationships that may lead to innovative partnerships or collaborations.

The journey to enhancing productivity through technology requires a proactive attitude and an open mind towards new developments. By following industry leaders, engaging in continuous learning, experimenting with new tools, and networking within professional circles, individuals can position themselves to take full advantage of technological advancements. This multi-faceted approach ensures not only increased efficiency but also growth in personal and professional capacities.

Being updated on emerging technologies isn't just about knowing what's new but understanding how these innovations can be practically applied to solve real-world challenges. Industry leaders and influencers share unique insights gained from hands-on experience, shedding light on potential pitfalls and success stories. They also provide practical advice on how to integrate new tools into existing systems, which is invaluable for anyone aiming to streamline operations. Therefore, actively engaging with this community through social media not only keeps you informed but also connects you with experts whose experiences can guide your own technology adoption journey.

Continuous learning through online courses and webinars is critical because technology evolves rapidly. What is cutting-edge today might become obsolete tomorrow. Hence, cultivating a habit of lifelong learning is crucial. Platforms like Coursera, Udemy, and edX offer courses led by experts from top institutions that cover a wide range of subjects. This diversity allows learners to broaden their skill sets, adapt to changes, and apply new techniques to improve productivity. A practical guideline for incorporating continuous learning is to set specific goals for what you want to achieve, whether it's gaining a new certification or mastering a particular tool, and then tracking your progress over time.

Trial testing software is another vital step in intelligently adopting new technologies. It minimizes risk since there is no initial financial investment, allowing users to try before they buy. This hands-on approach means that you can play around with the settings, understand the capabilities, and evaluate compatibility with your current processes. After testing, reflect on the experience: Did the software meet your expectations? Was it intuitive? Such reflection can guide informed purchasing decisions that align perfectly with productivity goals.

Building connections through professional groups and forums is similarly indispensable for fostering innovation. These communities serve as breeding grounds for shared learning and idea-generation. By interacting with other professionals who face similar challenges or work in the same sector, inspirations for implementing or adapting technology solutions can emerge. Additionally, being part of such a network enhances visibility and reputation within your field, potentially opening doors to new opportunities and collaborations.

The Bottom Line

As we've explored in this chapter, effectively using technology goes beyond mere adaptation; it's about finding the right fit that meshes seamlessly with individual work styles. Identifying tools that cater to one's specific needs can lead to a marked increase in productivity and efficiency. By taking a closer look at personal workflows and experimenting with different options, individuals can unveil new ways to streamline processes—whether through automating mundane tasks or adopting innovative scheduling solutions. This targeted approach encourages professionals to harness digital capabilities and make informed decisions, ultimately optimizing their daily activities.

Embracing efficient digital organization techniques further underscores the importance of structure and clarity in both professional and personal settings. Organizing digital resources, setting up task management systems, and creating focused workspaces contribute significantly to minimizing stress and enhancing productivity. As digital landscapes evolve, so too should our strategies to manage them effectively. Whether you're starting out in the workforce, seeking renewed motivation mid-career, or leading a principled business, these practices offer valuable insights into sustaining and elevating productivity. Preparing for future trends by staying updated and continuously learning ensures that technological advancements serve as allies on the path to success.

Chapter 20

What's Love Got to Do with It?

Exploring the Dimensions of Love

Instead of 'Love others as much as you love yourself.', love yourself unconditionally first, so you can be able to truly love all your environment's beauty and others. No one can give something that they don't have. **- The Author**

Imagine yourself running a marathon without properly lacing your shoes; you might have the stamina, but without the love and care in your preparation, you'll end up stumbling along the way— so lace up with love, and you'll cross the finish line with grace!

Exploring the dimensions of love opens a fascinating window into the various ways this powerful emotion shapes our interactions and relationships. Love isn't just one-dimensional; it ebbs and flows through different forms, adding layers of complexity to human connections. From romantic entanglements to the bonds of friendship, each type presents its unique characteristics and challenges, threading together the stories of our lives. This journey through love's landscape is essential for understanding not only how we interact with others but also how we perceive ourselves within those interactions. The diverse expressions of love influence not just personal relationships, but professional ones, too, providing insights that are invaluable in both realms.

In this chapter, we'll delve into several distinct types of love, each playing a crucial role in our emotional development and social fabric. You'll discover passionate *Eros*, which ignites fiery romance, and the selfless *Agape*, rooted in unconditional compassion. We'll also navigate through *Philia*, the affectionate bond of true friendship, and *Pragma*, the mature love epitomized by lasting commitment. You'll also encounter the playful and flirtatious Ludus, the vital essence of self-love in Philautia, and the warm, familial connection of Storge. Alongside these, we will explore the nuances of obsessive *Mania*, highlighting its risks and repercussions in relationships. By examining these different facets of love, you'll gain insights into how they contribute to healthier, more fulfilling connections and learn strategies to cultivate them in your own life. Whether you're a young professional, a mid-career individual, or an aspiring leader, understanding these elements will empower you to foster strong, meaningful relationships personally and professionally.

Understanding EROS: Passionate and Romantic Love

Eros, often associated with passionate love, carries a powerful force of attraction and intense emotions. It's the kind of love where people feel swept off their feet, thrilled by the very presence of their partner. This type of love can manifest as a strong physical attraction, blending emotional intensity with a deep need for connection. When individuals experience Eros, they might feel a rush of excitement and an invigorating pull towards their loved one, which often feels both inevitable and thrilling.

In romantic relationships, Eros plays a crucial role, acting as the initial spark that ignites desire and interest between partners. It fuels the early stages of love with passion and enthusiasm, helping to create a vibrant bond. However, while this passionate love is essential, it's equally important to strike a balance between passion and stability. Without balance, relationships can fall victim to volatility or even turbulence, driven by unchecked emotions and unrealistic expectations.

Identifying the right equilibrium involves understanding that while passion is a vital component, it needs grounding in mutual respect and trust. Stability doesn't mean suppressing passion; rather, it's about nurturing a relationship where both partners feel secure enough to express themselves honestly. By focusing on communication and shared values, couples can lay a foundation that supports enduring love beyond the initial thrill of Eros.

For those who find the flames of Eros flickering, there are techniques to rekindle this passion in their relationships. First, investing time in shared experiences can build layers of intimacy and refresh the sense of closeness. Trying new activities together, planning surprise dates, or simply being present for each other can reignite that initial spark. Another method is revisiting cherished memories or reliving moments from the beginning of the relationship, which can renew affection and appreciation.

Moreover, fostering an atmosphere where curiosity and admiration thrive helps keep Eros alive. Partners should be encouraged to continue exploring aspects of each other's personalities, interests, and dreams. This ongoing discovery can fuel passion, reminding each person why they were drawn to each other in the first place. Keeping the lines of communication open ensures that both partners remain aware of each other's evolving needs and desires, allowing love to adapt and grow over time.

Acknowledging that passion evolves is crucial for appreciating love as a dynamic process. Relationships are not static; they change as individuals grow and navigate life's challenges. Understanding this evolution can shift perspective, prompting partners to embrace changes as opportunities to deepen their connection. Recognizing that the nature of Eros may transform into something more profound allows couples to see love's potential for resilience and adaptation.

Embracing change can also mitigate conflicts arising from unmet expectations. If passion wanes, some might erroneously believe the love has diminished. However, love can take different forms, moving gracefully from an urgent, desirous feeling to a steadier, intimate bond. Couples willing to acknowledge this transformation can more readily weather periods of reduced passion without questioning the strength of their relationship.

Open discussions about evolving feelings can help reinforce the relationship's foundation, turning changes into chances for shared growth rather than signs of failure. Partners should aim to support each other through life's transitions, whether they're dealing with career shifts, family responsibilities, or personal development. By doing so, they can maintain a healthy partnership that honors both individual aspirations and collective goals.

Understanding Eros also involves recognizing its vulnerabilities. While this type of love is exhilarating, it can lead to emotional highs and lows if left unchecked. The intensity can result in possessiveness or dependency, straining the relationship. Navigating these challenges involves self-awareness and reflection, ensuring that passionate love remains a source of joy rather than distress.

Educating oneself about Eros' nature prepares individuals to enter relationships with realistic expectations. By embracing both the joys and challenges of passionate love, people can navigate their romantic lives more effectively. As they grow more attuned to their emotions and the dynamics of their relationships, they'll be better equipped to create fulfilling romantic partnerships that thrive over time.

The Selfless Nature of AGAPE: Unconditional Love and Compassion

Agape love, a concept often celebrated for its selfless and unconditional nature, holds the potential to transform relationships in profound ways. Characterized by altruism, Agape is about fostering connections through compassion and empathy, fundamentally changing how we interact with others. Unlike other types of love, which might be based on shared experiences or romantic attachment, Agape is unconditional, often described as the most selfless form of love.

At the heart of Agape lies the commitment to act with kindness and understanding, even when it requires personal sacrifice. Imagine a busy professional who takes time out of their hectic schedule to volunteer at a local shelter. Their actions are not driven by a desire for recognition but by a genuine wish to make a positive impact on the lives of those less fortunate. Such concrete actions amplify the essence of Agape, showcasing its significance in our day-to-day interactions. This type of love pushes us to go beyond ourselves, encouraging acts of empathy that can strengthen our bonds with family, friends, and even strangers.

In daily life, demonstrating Agape can be as simple as listening intently to someone in need or offering support without expecting anything in return. These gestures, although small, weave a fabric of connection and reinforce the importance of compassion in our interactions. They serve as reminders that love is not just a feeling but an action—a deliberate choice to put another's well-being ahead of our own desires or convenience.

However, practicing Agape is not without its challenges. The modern world often emphasizes individual achievement and personal gain, creating barriers to the cultivation of such selfless love. Recognizing these barriers is crucial for developing more nurturing relationships. For instance, societal norms might pressure individuals to prioritize their careers over personal relationships, sometimes leading to isolation or strained connections. By acknowledging these obstacles, we can work towards overcoming them, making room for deeper, more meaningful connections enriched by Agape.

The practice of Agape also plays a critical role in cultivating patience and understanding—traits essential for nurturing healthy relationships. Consider the impact of this love in a workplace setting, where teamwork and collaboration are vital. When leaders approach their teams with Agape, they foster an environment of trust and respect. Employees feel valued and supported, knowing that their well-being is appreciated alongside their contributions. In turn, this nurtures loyalty and encourages a positive, productive culture.

Developing Agape requires patience and perseverance. It asks us to look beyond immediate gratifications, focusing instead on long-term harmony and mutual growth. A parent, for example, practices Agape by consistently guiding and supporting their child through the ups and downs of life. The parent's patience, alongside their understanding of the child's unique experiences, strengthens the bond and lays the foundation for a resilient relationship.

For young professionals entering the workforce, embracing Agape can enhance their leadership skills. It encourages them to lead with empathy, striving to understand the perspectives and challenges of their colleagues. This approach not only fosters team cohesion but also helps in building a reputation as a thoughtful, inclusive leader. Similarly, mid-career individuals seeking transformation can find renewed motivation by integrating Agape into their personal and professional lives. By prioritizing compassion over competition, they can navigate stagnant periods with optimism and resilience, ultimately driving positive change in their careers and personal development.

Entrepreneurs and aspiring leaders also stand to benefit significantly from practicing Agape. By building businesses rooted in ethical practices, they create workplaces where employees thrive. This fosters a culture of mutual respect and cooperation, aligning everyone towards common goals. Through selfless leadership, they empower their teams, inspiring commitment and innovation that propel the organization forward.

While the journey towards practicing Agape may seem daunting due to its demanding nature, the rewards are undeniably transformative. Embracing this form of love leads to profound personal growth, expanding one's capacity for empathy and understanding. As we become more adept at seeing the world through others' eyes, our ability to communicate and connect deeply with people is enhanced, paving the way for fulfilling relationships both personally and professionally.

Cultivating PHILIA: The Affectionate Bond of Friendship

Philia, often described as a deep love of friendship, represents some of the strongest connections in our lives. This type of love is rooted in loyalty and shared experiences that weave the fabric of enduring relationships. Friendship, through philia, becomes a space where individuals support one another through life's journey, providing emotional fortitude and companionship. The ancient Greeks viewed philia not just as camaraderie but as an integral part of achieving personal fulfillment and mutual respect among peers.

In today's fast-paced world, recognizing the value of quality over quantity in friendships is paramount. While having many acquaintances may seem appealing, it's the depth of connection with a few cherished friends that truly matters. These longstanding bonds offer significant emotional support. In times of stress or uncertainty, having someone who genuinely understands your struggles can be comforting. This kind of emotional backing plays a critical role in mental well-being, allowing us to navigate life's challenges with resilience.

Friendships built on philia act as buffers against stress and emotional turmoil, providing a sanctuary for honest expression. Imagine facing a tough day at work or dealing with personal setbacks; during such times, knowing there are friends to lean on can make all the difference. Their presence helps mitigate feelings of isolation, encouraging openness and vulnerability in a safe environment. Strong friendships furnish us with a network of support, enhancing our capacity to face adversities.

As we move further into the digital age, the nature of friendship is evolving. Online interactions now form a significant portion of how we connect with others. Understanding this shift is crucial to maintaining genuine connections. Digital platforms offer opportunities for communication beyond geographical constraints, fostering relationships that might not otherwise exist. However, these online interactions can sometimes lack the depth of real-life connections if not cultivated mindfully. Navigating this landscape requires discernment to ensure our digital engagements supplement rather than detract from authentic bonds.

The potential pitfalls of online friendships include superficial connections, where interactions remain on the surface without the depth required for true philia. To counter this, it's important to nurture online friendships with the same intentionality as we would in-person ones. Engaging in meaningful conversations, sharing personal stories, and offering real-time support are ways to enrich digital friendships. Being selective about which interactions we invest time in will help ensure they contribute positively to our emotional lives.

Moreover, transitioning online friendships into offline experiences when possible can strengthen these bonds further. Meeting a friend you've known only online can deepen your understanding of each other, solidifying the connection through shared experiences. This blend of virtual and physical interaction can embody the essence of philia, merging the convenience of technology with the authenticity of face-to-face contact.

Building strong friendships doesn't happen overnight. It involves dedication, time, and a genuine interest in each other's lives. Investing in friendships by regularly checking in and planning activities together solidifies bonds. Simple gestures like remembering significant dates or milestones show that you care, reinforcing loyalty and trust—the hallmarks of philia. As friends celebrate each other's successes or provide comfort in challenging times, they create a positive feedback loop that enhances overall well-being.

For young professionals entering the workforce, forging true friendships can be invaluable. Such connections provide support and encouragement, especially in high-pressure environments. Mid-career individuals, too, benefit from nurturing these bonds to combat stagnation and find renewed motivation. For entrepreneurs and aspiring leaders, cultivating genuine friendships translates into stronger team dynamics and a supportive workplace culture, which is essential for achieving business success.

Navigating PRAGMA: Mature and Enduring Love

Pragma, a term derived from the Greek word for "pragmatic," is a love built on longevity and practicality. Unlike the fiery rush of youthful romance, Pragma embodies a mature affection grounded in steadfast commitment and mutual understanding. For many, it's what transforms relationships from transient to timeless, providing a foundation that withstands the tests of life.

At the heart of Pragma is the deep-rooted belief that love is as much about functionality as it is about feeling. This form of love sees partners standing by each other through life's ebbs and flows, showcasing a dedication that goes beyond fleeting passion. Such a connection requires continuous nurturing through open communication and negotiation, which are essential components in sustaining a lasting partnership over time. As one navigates daily challenges, it's this open dialogue that helps clarify expectations, align goals, and resolve misunderstandings before they burgeon into resentment.

To ensure the enduring nature of Pragma, the role of compromise cannot be overstated. Flexibility is the essence of this love type, as it demands that individuals willingly bend and adapt not just for their benefit but for the relationship's collective good. In practice, compromise might involve adjusting personal goals to accommodate shared dreams or finding a middle ground on differing worldviews. This dynamic adaptability underscores the resilience of Pragma, allowing couples to grow together rather than drift apart when faced with change or adversity.

One powerful way pragmatic love manifests itself is through shared ventures and interests. These joint activities can serve as a crucible for growth, providing couples with unique opportunities to deepen their emotional bonds. Whether it's embarking on a business venture or pursuing a hobby together, such shared experiences can fortify the relationship by promoting teamwork, reinforcing trust, and enhancing understanding. It's not merely about spending time together, but about creating meaningful interactions that contribute to mutual development and satisfaction.

An interesting perspective on Pragma is its initial perception as unromantic or overly practical. There's a notion that this type of love lacks excitement, yet dismissing it would overlook its true depth and potential. While it may lack the explosive thrill associated with the initial attraction, Pragma offers something more valuable—a steady companionship that fuels love's longevity. Over time, the spark of infatuation gives way to a profound respect and recognition of one's partner as an ally in life's journey.

Research also suggests that relationships exemplifying Pragma are often those that have survived the fervent beginnings marked by Eros and evolved under the patient guidance of time. The transition from passionate love to pragmatic love isn't a loss but a transformation—an evolution that brings stability and peace. This transformation involves recognizing that the person beside us is integral to our story, one whose strengths and weaknesses are accepted without judgment.

Indeed, embracing Pragma means committing to love as an active choice rather than a passive state of being. It's not about waiting for the euphoria to hit but diligently working to keep the bond alive. By seeing love as a practice, couples engage in acts that reaffirm their loyalty and dedication consistently. This thoughtful approach to love requires mindfulness and presence, encouraging partners to appreciate daily interactions' nuances and subtleties.

However, the journey towards achieving Pragma isn't always straightforward. It might demand unlearning certain romanticized notions of love portrayed in media and culture. It asks individuals to redefine what constitutes a successful and fulfilling relationship by focusing less on grand gestures and more on everyday acts of kindness, patience, and empathy. In this light, the gifts of Pragma become evident—not only is it a testament to the power of enduring love, but it also provides a blueprint for how two people can harmoniously navigate life's complexities together.

For those young professionals entering the workforce or mid-career individuals seeking renewed motivation, Pragma serves as a reminder of the importance of stability and support in personal and professional relationships. By adopting principles of honesty, patience, and dedication characteristic of Pragma, they can foster strong partnerships both at home and in their careers. Entrepreneurs and aspiring leaders might find inspiration in Pragma's lessons, applying them to cultivate principled businesses where collaboration and shared vision drive success.

Understanding LUDUS: Playful and Flirtatious Love

Ludus, the playful type of love, embodies a sense of joy and spontaneity that characterizes the early stages of romantic interactions. It thrives on the exhilaration that comes from flirtation, teasing, and the excitement of newfound connections. In many ways, Ludus is the embodiment of the thrill of the chase, where partners engage in playful banter and lighthearted activities that foster attraction without the weight of serious commitments. This type of love allows individuals to explore their romantic interests in a carefree manner, facilitating a dynamic exchange that can lead to deeper connections.

One of the most intriguing aspects of Ludus is its focus on enjoyment rather than obligation. In this stage, partners may enjoy casual dates, spontaneous adventures, and playful challenges that add a layer of excitement to their interactions. The light tone of Ludus can serve as a form of emotional relief, enabling individuals to escape the pressures of daily life and simply enjoy being in the moment with someone special. Whether it's through shared laughs, adventurous outings, or mischievous gestures, the essence of Ludus lies in creating cherished memories filled with joy.

Despite its predominantly jubilant nature, Ludus raises important questions about dating and relationships. While the playful aspects can be exhilarating, individuals must recognize the potential risks associated with remaining in this stage for too long. Prolonged engagement in Ludus may lead to an avoidance of deeper emotional connections or a reluctance to commit seriously. It's important for partners to evaluate their intentions and communicate openly about their desires for the relationship to avoid creating confusion or hurt feelings later on.

A significant component of Ludus is the role of emotional and psychological boundaries. In a playful relationship, partners often need to navigate their emotional security carefully to prevent misunderstandings or insecurities. It's crucial to maintain trust while engaging in lighthearted interactions. Clear communication about the nature of the relationship can help ensure that both individuals are on the same page, thereby cultivating a positive and enjoyable experience.

Furthermore, Ludus can help individuals develop important social skills that will benefit them in future relationships. Through playful interactions, individuals learn how to read social cues, navigate romantic tension, and cultivate a sense of charm. These skills can serve as building blocks for more serious relationships down the road. By embracing the spirit of Ludus, people can tap into their creative and playful sides, enriching their dating experience.

In relationships marked by Ludus, mutual respect is essential. While the playful nature often mitigates the pressure of expectations, partners must be attentive to each other's feelings. Laughing together should never come at the expense of someone's emotional well-being. Demonstrating empathy and understanding can enhance the playful dynamic without crossing boundaries.

Ludus also encourages the exploration of personal interests. Partners can engage in new activities together, enrich their experiences, and discover shared passions. Whether it's dancing, hiking, or playing games, Ludus emphasizes the importance of discovering joy in each other's company. As individuals partake in joyful experiences, they deepen their connection while keeping the spirit of adventure alive.

Ultimately, Ludus serves as a refreshing entry point to the complex world of love. It embodies the excitement and freedom that can come with romantic exploration, allowing partners to connect in delightful and meaningful ways. Embracing the playful nature of Ludus can provide individuals with lasting memories and connections, laying the groundwork for deeper types of love in the future.

Embracing PHILAUTIA: The Importance of Self-Love

Philautia, or self-love, is a foundational type of love that emphasizes the significance of nurturing one's own well-being. In a world where societal pressures often encourage self-criticism or comparison, recognizing the value of self-love can transform how individuals relate not only to themselves but also to others. At its core, Philautia promotes a healthy sense of self-worth, encouraging individuals to embrace their unique qualities, strengths, and imperfections.

Engaging in self-love involves prioritizing self-care and self-compassion. This practice allows individuals to create a healthy relationship with themselves, fostering emotional stability and resilience. By understanding and accepting their worth, individuals can cultivate a powerful bond within that becomes the basis for engaging with others. Philautia not only helps mitigate feelings of inadequacy but also empowers individuals to pursue their passions and aspirations with confidence.

Realizing the importance of self-love can be particularly transformative for personal growth. When individuals practice Philautia, they often find that they are more open to setting boundaries and advocating for their needs. This newfound assertiveness nurtures relationships and fosters mutual respect, encouraging individuals to surround themselves with people who appreciate and validate their individuality. Strong self-love lays the groundwork for healthier interactions with friends, family, and partners.

Philautia also invites individuals to challenge negative thought patterns that can lead to self-doubt. By embracing self-acceptance, individuals can dismantle the barriers created by harsh self-judgment. This transformative journey often involves cultivating a positive inner dialogue, taking the time to celebrate achievements, big or small, and recognizing personal growth. Engaging in activities that nourish the soul can further enhance this connection with oneself, fostering a deep sense of fulfillment.

One of the notable outcomes of practicing Philautia is the ripple effect it can have on relationships. As individuals nurture their self-love, they become more adept at loving and supporting others. The strength derived from one's own self-acceptance empowers them to create positive, loving environments, positively influencing interactions with family, friends, and partners. When individuals embody self-love, they often find themselves more equipped to offer genuine care and compassion to others without the risk of emotional depletion.

However, it's crucial to acknowledge that self-love is not synonymous with narcissism. Philautia encourages individuals to prioritize their own well-being while remaining attuned to the needs of those around them. The balance between healthy self-love and thoughtful consideration for others fosters empathy and connection, contributing to harmonious relationships. Practicing Philautia responsibly allows individuals to love themselves while building meaningful connections.

In a professional context, self-love can be a powerful catalyst for success. When individuals value themselves, they are more likely to pursue opportunities and advocate for their needs in the workplace. This assertiveness fosters confidence and encourages individuals to chase their passions, align their work with their values, and establish boundaries that promote work-life balance. As a result, professionals who embrace Philautia are often more fulfilled in their careers.

To practice Philautia, individuals might engage in activities that promote self-reflection and personal growth. Journaling, meditation, or seeking therapeutic support are valuable tools for individuals on their journey to embrace self-love. Additionally, surrounding oneself with supportive and uplifting communities fosters an environment where self-love flourishes, allowing individuals to thrive emotionally and socially.

Ultimately, Philautia highlights the integral role of self-love in fulfilling relationships. By recognizing the importance of loving oneself, individuals enrich their connections with others, fostering an environment where love can thrive. Celebrating one's individuality and cultivating a positive self-relationship becomes an essential part of navigating the complexities of love in both personal and professional spheres.

Exploring STORGE: *Affectionate and Familial Love*

Storge represents the affection that blooms in familial and platonic relationships, characterized by deep-seated love, loyalty, and companionship. This type of love often develops naturally over time as individuals forge connections based on shared experiences and mutual support. Storge emphasizes the importance of emotional bonds cultivated through familiarity, highlighting the ease with which strong connections can be formed among family members and close friends.

At the core of Storge lies a profound sense of security and belonging. Relationships characterized by Storge are built on a foundation of trust, where individuals feel safe to express their feelings and navigate life's trials together. This nurturing love fosters an environment where emotional vulnerability is welcomed and valued, enabling individuals to share their joys and sorrows authentically without fear of judgment. Such intimacy strengthens the emotional fabric of relationships and creates lasting memories that individuals cherish throughout their lives.

In families, Storge plays a pivotal role in shaping emotional development. Parents often express Storge through unconditional love, providing children with a stable environment to grow and explore their identities. This affectionate bond instills a sense of worth and security, equipping individuals to form healthy relationships later in life. Sibling relationships also exemplify Storge, where shared experiences create a unique bond characterized by loyalty, camaraderie, and mutual support.

Storge extends beyond familial connections; it encompasses the lasting friendships that individuals cultivate over the years. Close friends who embody Storge often become chosen family, embodying deep affection, reliability, and unwavering support. These friendships are marked by shared experiences, celebrations, and mutual understanding, creating a sanctuary for emotional expression. In times of need, friends who embody Storge provide comfort, companionship, and a listening ear, reinforcing the significance of meaningful connections.

While Storge is inherently nurturing, it also poses challenges. Long-term relationships can become complacent, leading to a reliance on familiarity that may stifle growth or emotional exploration. Partners should actively engage in open communication, sharing their thoughts and feelings to ensure the relationship remains dynamic and fulfilling. Cultivating interests together and creating new experiences can reignite the emotional spark, helping individuals navigate life's complexities while maintaining a sense of adventure.

Another rewarding aspect of Storge is the power of shared values and beliefs. When individuals bond over common interests, ideals, or passions, their connection deepens, reinforcing their commitment to one another. A shared sense of purpose can motivate individuals to support each other's goals, fostering an environment of encouragement and growth where each person thrives personally and professionally.

Moreover, Storge can serve as a strong foundation for romantic relationships. As friendships evolve into romantic connections, the presence of Storge can enhance emotional intimacy and commitment. When individuals transition from friends to partners, they carry the emotional trust and understanding that has developed over time, resulting in a more profound and resilient bond. Such relationships often flourish because partners have built an authentic connection grounded in affection and familiarity.

Storge reminds us that love doesn't always have to be passionate or intense; it can instead be a steady, nurturing force that provides comfort and security. It is a love that perseveres through challenges and fosters deep, lasting connections. By appreciating the essence of Storge, individuals can cultivate emotional resilience, understanding that strong relationships are built on love that transcends life's ups and downs.

In summary, Storge represents the affectionate love that forms the backbone of our relationships, encompassing familial bonds, friendships, and deeper connections. The nurturing nature of Storge emphasizes the significance of emotional security, loyalty, and shared experiences, reminding us that the love we cultivate can profoundly impact our lives. Encouraging open communication, shared adventures, and mutual support can further enrich these connections, allowing individuals to navigate the complexities of love with grace and understanding.

Avoiding the MANIA: The Obsessive Love

Love, often celebrated for its beauty and power to unite, also possesses a shadowy side that can lead individuals down darker paths of obsession and dependency. Understanding this facet of love is crucial as it sheds light on behaviors that, while initially cloaked in romance, can intrude upon personal well-being and the health of relationships.

The rollercoaster of intense emotional highs and lows typifies this kind of obsessive love. It mirrors the pull of addiction, where moments of euphoria are followed by crashing lows. Imagine the thrill of your partner's laughter, and the comfort of their scent, which feels like pure bliss. However, this joy can quickly turn to anxiety when they seem distant or unresponsive. Such fluctuations can deeply affect daily life, leaving one constantly at the mercy of emotions. This unstable state isn't just mentally taxing; it seeps into physical health, affecting sleep, appetite, and even cardiovascular functions, emphasizing how such entanglements stretch far beyond the heart's domain.

Possessiveness emerges as another stark characteristic of obsessive love. This excessive need to 'own' another person can morph into destructive doubt and insecurity. When a partner constantly questions their loved one's fidelity or intentions, it sows seeds of mistrust. This cycle is dangerous, creating an environment where accusations become frequent, leading to arguments and increased emotional distance. As partners grow wary of each other, suspicion replaces understanding, and fear of betrayal looms large. This insecurity doesn't just impact the person feeling it but also burdens the relationship with undue stress and conflict, diminishing its core essence.

Recognizing healthy dedication to unhealthy needs forms a pivotal step toward healing. Dedication in love means standing by someone, nurturing mutual growth, and respecting individuality. In contrast, unhealthy need demands constant assurance and sacrifice of personal boundaries. It's critical to understand that love shouldn't dismantle one's identity or lead them to seek validation exclusively from their partner. Instead, healthy love respects autonomy and promotes self-worth. By acknowledging these boundaries, individuals can navigate their feelings more clearly, aiming for a balanced relationship that uplifts rather than confines.

Self-reflection plays an indispensable role in understanding and overcoming obsessive patterns. Taking the time to introspect what triggers these feelings of obsession can offer profound insights. Perhaps past experiences, ingrained fears, or unmet needs fuel such dependencies. By exploring these areas, individuals gain clarity on their behavior, allowing them to address underlying issues rather than just managing symptoms. Techniques like journaling, meditation, or professional counseling can aid in this journey, helping detach emotional responses from automatic reactions. By recognizing these patterns, individuals not only enhance their self-awareness but also pave the way toward healthier relational dynamics.

Such an understanding of obsession and dependency on love has been backed by significant research. In my own life and my relationships, I had a few opportunities to realize how love addiction aligns with mental health struggles like anxiety and depression, illustrating that these aren't mere phases but genuine challenges requiring attention. Similarly, I am qualified to emphasize how intense attachments can mimic behavioral addictions, underscoring the importance of viewing these romantic entanglements through a nuanced lens. These insights highlight the necessity of approaching love not just as an emotion, but as a complex interplay of needs, desires, and behaviors.

To those grappling with obsessive tendencies, it's essential to remember that seeking help is a sign of strength, not weakness. Professional therapies offer tools and strategies tailored to unravel such complexities, aiding individuals in building resilience against these consuming feelings. Furthermore, fostering self-love acts as a powerful antidote. By embracing oneself with compassion and care, the dependency on external validation diminishes. Cultivating interests outside of the relationship, engaging in hobbies, or fostering friendships can provide fulfilling avenues for joy and satisfaction, reducing the burden placed on romantic relationships for fulfillment.

Final Insights

Exploring the varied forms of love reveals their profound significance in our lives and relationships. We've journeyed through Eros, appreciating its passionate beginnings and understanding the need for balance to maintain stability. Agape's selflessness teaches us how altruism can transform our interactions, while Philia emphasizes the cherished bonds of friendship that offer emotional resilience. In recognizing Pragma, we uncover the beauty of mature love, where commitment and practicality pave the way for enduring partnerships. Additionally, the playful nature of Ludus reminds us to embrace joy and flirtation in our relationships, while Philautia emphasizes the importance of self-love as a foundation for connecting with others. Storge highlights the warm, familial love that nurtures our emotional well-being. Meanwhile, staying mindful of Mania ensures that we approach love with a healthy perspective, avoiding the pitfalls of obsession and dependency. Together, these insights provide a comprehensive guide to navigating love's complexities in both personal and professional life.

As you move through your career or personal journeys, acknowledging these diverse aspects of love can enrich your experiences and relationships. Whether you are stepping into the workforce, seeking growth in your career, or building a principled business, understanding how each form of love influences human connection will empower you to foster meaningful, supportive environments. Love, in its many shapes, isn't just a private matter; it profoundly impacts how we lead, connect with others, and drive positive change. By weaving love's principles into your actions and decisions, you'll be better equipped to thrive and inspire those around you.

Chapter 21

Reflecting on the Journey to Excellence

Excellence is not merely a destination, but a continuous journey fueled by an open heart, where each moment of reflection illuminates our path and fosters an attitude of growth and improvement. **- The Author**

Imagine yourself looking back at a road trip; you might laugh at the wrong turns and forget the snacks, but each pit stop and scenic overlook adds flavor to the experience, making you appreciate the journey even more than the final destination!

Reflecting on the journey to excellence requires a steadfast commitment to self-improvement and acute awareness of one's progress. This chapter explores how reflection becomes a bridge linking past experiences with future aspirations, allowing individuals to harness their history as a guide for what lies ahead. Whether it is marking achievements or learning from challenges, reflection serves as a powerful tool to propel personal and professional growth. Through introspection, professionals can celebrate milestones that fuel motivation and pride, encouraging them not only to acknowledge what has been accomplished but also to recognize the potential for further advancement.

The chapter delves into practical strategies to enhance reflective practices effectively. It begins by underscoring the importance of recognizing accomplishments and drawing lessons from past experiences. We will discover methods to document these experiences in a manner that provides tangible evidence of growth, fostering a continuous narrative of progress. Furthermore, the discussion includes techniques for integrating feedback from peers and mentors, ensuring diverse perspectives enrich the development process. The narrative emphasizes that this reflective journey is not solely about looking back; it is about paving the way forward with clarity and confidence, thereby setting well-informed goals that align with evolving priorities. Through this lens, we will gain insights into utilizing reflection to navigate their career paths with intentionality and purpose, ultimately leading them toward excellence.

Assessing Accomplishments and Lessons Learned

Reflecting on the journey to excellence involves recognizing the milestones that mark progress along the way. Every step forward and significant achievement contributes to personal and professional growth. These milestones, whether large or small, serve as powerful reminders of our journey's positive aspects. For young professionals, acknowledging these achievements can cultivate a sense of pride and motivation, reinforcing a positive self-image crucial for building confidence in their burgeoning careers.

Analyzing challenges is another critical aspect of reflecting on past experiences. Each obstacle encountered and overcome offers invaluable lessons, enhancing resilience and sharpening problem-solving skills. By examining hurdles faced in the past, individuals can identify patterns, adjust strategies, and ultimately emerge stronger and more adaptable. This process is about learning from mistakes and developing a mindset that views challenges as opportunities for growth. It's particularly beneficial for mid-career individuals looking to rejuvenate their professional lives by seeing previous setbacks as stepping stones rather than stumbling blocks.

Documenting experiences is an effective practice for maintaining a tangible record of progress. Keeping journals or digital records of both successes and failures allows individuals to revisit past experiences with fresh perspectives. This documentation acts as a source of insights and encouragement, reminding us of our resilience and capacity to overcome adversity. Beyond mere records, these documents provide an opportunity to examine growth over time, recognize patterns, and celebrate the victories that helped shape one's career path. In this pursuit, it's helpful to establish a guideline. Consider setting aside regular intervals for documenting updates, reflections, and observations to maintain a comprehensive account of your journey.

Feedback reflection further aids in personal growth by integrating external perspectives into one's learning process. Gathering insights from peers, mentors, and colleagues provides essential viewpoints that might not be visible from a solitary perspective. Constructive feedback allows individuals to understand how they are perceived by others, which can affirm strengths and identify areas needing improvement. It encourages open dialogue and fosters an environment where continuous improvement is valued. For entrepreneurs and leaders, this practice can build stronger teams and cultivate a workplace culture rooted in mutual respect and development. Establishing routine channels for receiving feedback—whether through scheduled reviews or informal conversations—ensures that diverse insights are incorporated consistently into personal development strategies.

By focusing on these elements of reflection, individuals across various stages of their careers can recognize achievements and learn from every experience. Highlighting milestones fortifies motivation, while analyzing challenges refines problem-solving capacities. Documenting experiences ensures the continuity of personal history and provides a chronicle of growth. Lastly, feedback reflection integrates valuable external perspectives, enriching the development process. Together, these practices form a robust framework for ongoing personal and professional advancement, guiding individuals toward excellence with greater clarity and purpose.

Adjusting Goals Based on Current Insights

Reflecting on the journey to excellence necessitates the refinement of goals with new knowledge and experiences. For young professionals and mid-career individuals, reassessing values can help align personal and career objectives with their evolving priorities. As life progresses, so do our beliefs and aspirations. This evolution is a natural process that requires conscious reflection and adjustment. By periodically reviewing what you value most—whether it be family, career growth, or community involvement—you ensure your goals remain meaningful and inspiring. For example, a young professional might initially focus on rapid career advancement but later realize that a balanced lifestyle brings more fulfillment. As such, reassessing and realigning goals with these updated values supports long-term satisfaction and purpose.

Utilizing the SMART framework in goal setting is another effective strategy for refining your aspirations amid change. Goals should be Specific, Measurable, Achievable, Relevant, and Time-bound. Revisiting and adjusting your goals to fit this model ensures they are precise and realistic, providing a clear roadmap for achievement. Consider an entrepreneur who aims to launch a new product line. Initially, the goal may simply be to expand the business. However, breaking it down into SMART components allows for targeted actions: defining a launch date (Time-bound), estimating projected sales (Measurable), ensuring resources are available (Achievable), and aligning the launch with company values (Relevant). Such clarity helps track progress while accommodating shifts in the market or personal circumstances.

Creating new challenges is essential for pushing beyond comfort zones and achieving greater potential. While comfort may offer temporary ease, true growth often lies in the unfamiliar. By intentionally setting ambitious yet attainable goals, individuals are motivated to develop new skills and explore uncharted territories.

For instance, a mid-career professional stagnating in their role might set a challenge to lead a high-profile project or pursue further education. These challenges not only promote self-improvement but also boost confidence and resilience. Additionally, embracing new opportunities paves the way for innovation and creative problem-solving, vital attributes for both personal and professional success.

The importance of maintaining a feedback loop cannot be overstated. Routine reflection and seeking feedback are integral for accountability and progressive learning. Engaging with peers, mentors, and self-assessment practices provides diverse perspectives that enrich understanding and growth. Feedback helps identify strengths and uncover areas needing improvement, making it invaluable for continuous development. For aspiring leaders, cultivating a culture of open communication encourages team members to contribute their insights, thus enhancing collective performance. In this context, reflections become collaborative efforts that align individual and group aspirations, fostering an environment where everyone thrives.

Incorporating these strategies into your routine fortifies the journey towards excellence by maintaining a dynamic approach to personal and professional development. As young professionals, mid-career individuals, and entrepreneurs navigate varied pathways, the ability to adapt and refine objectives becomes crucial. By consistently reassessing values, applying the SMART framework, embracing challenges, and actively participating in feedback loops, you equip yourself with the tools necessary for sustained growth and achievement.

Imagine the impact of regularly practicing these approaches. Over time, small adjustments made through reflection and feedback culminate in significant transformations. Greater self-awareness and adaptability emerge as byproducts, allowing you to pivot seamlessly in the face of unexpected challenges. For instance, an entrepreneur who routinely revisits their goals and seeks feedback is better equipped to steer their business through economic fluctuations. Similarly, a young professional who continually aligns their aspirations with their core values remains motivated and engaged even as their career path evolves.

This commitment to reflection and adaptation empowers individuals to create meaningful forward momentum. Each experience, whether deemed successful or not, serves as a lesson, enriching the narrative of your journey. Embrace the process wholeheartedly, viewing each goal revision as an opportunity to redefine what excellence means to you. This mindset not only enhances personal fulfillment but also sets a precedent of lifelong learning—a cornerstone of leadership and influence in today's dynamic world.

Expressing Gratitude for Achievements

Gratitude is a powerful tool for reinforcing positive experiences, an invaluable asset in both personal and professional realms. Journaling about gratitude can act as a potent reminder of one's achievements, encouraging a positive long-term outlook. By regularly jotting down the things you're grateful for, you create an opportunity to reflect on progress and appreciate growth over time. This practice not only highlights patterns of advancement but also provides clarity during challenging times by reminding you of past successes.

Engaging in gratitude journaling offers a structured way to document these milestones. It can serve as a roadmap through your journey, capturing moments of success that might otherwise blend into daily routines. For example, a young professional might note the completion of an intricate project, while a mid-career individual could record achieving a work-life balance milestone. These entries build a portfolio of accomplishments that affirm potential and capability. As a Success Mentor for more than thirty years now, I may argue that practicing gratitude can boost happiness, resilience, and relationships, offering tangible life benefits.

Mapping out achievements in a journal allows for introspection into how far you've come. Equally important is sharing this sense of accomplishment with others. Acknowledging the help and collaboration from those around you strengthens bonds and fosters community. Sharing success stories doesn't just celebrate personal triumph but uplifts those who contributed. This communal aspect of gratitude underlines the interconnectedness in a workplace or social group, creating an environment where everyone feels valued.

The act of celebrating success collectively brings us to the idea of creating personal rituals. Whether it's a small treat after completing a task or a more elaborate celebration, building rituals to honor achievements can motivate continued effort. Celebratory rituals act as markers in our journey, providing a moment to pause and savor the fruits of dedication and hard work. For entrepreneurs or team leaders, instituting such practices within a company culture can enhance morale and loyalty.

Consider how successful sports teams celebrate victories. They engage in rituals like ringing bells or throwing confetti, embedding a culture of recognition and appreciation. These practices reinforce memorable moments and stimulate motivation across the board. As an aspiring leader, such celebrations can be pivotal in maintaining team spirit and driving collective goals forward.

Beyond these shared and solo practices, gratitude plays a crucial role in emotional well-being. Harnessing gratitude enhances positive emotions, which are foundational in building resilience. It's about shifting focus from shortcomings to strengths, nurturing a mindset that overcomes setbacks with grace and optimism. Throught my mentoring journeys I can suggest that gratitude acts as a muscle, developing with acknowledgment of life's favorable elements. By consistently practicing gratitude, individuals can maintain a balanced perspective, appreciating good times while being prepared to tackle challenges.

Incorporating gratitude into daily routines doesn't need to be overwhelming. Even small, mindful choices can yield significant impacts. For instance, starting each day by noting three things you're grateful for sets a positive tone and directs attention to what's thriving in life. Such habits can be cultivated alongside regular activities, forming an effortless part of your daily schedule.

Entrepreneurs and professionals can apply these gratitude practices to their business environments, too. Acknowledging team contributions during meetings or setting aside time monthly to reflect on shared achievements can enhance teamwork and improve productivity. According to my life experiences, gratitude is a straightforward yet beneficial tool that improves emotional health and promotes helpful, compassionate behavior in teams.

Moreover, by recognizing success and expressing gratitude in professional circles, you cultivate a workplace where appreciation becomes second nature. Employees feel more engaged, valued, and motivated to contribute when they see their efforts acknowledged. This culture of gratitude can drastically impact job satisfaction and retention, particularly for those entering the workforce seeking meaningful engagement.

Gratitude thus serves as a multi-faceted ally on the journey to excellence. By integrating gratitude journaling, sharing successes, establishing celebratory rituals, and reinforcing positive emotions, you create a robust framework supporting personal and professional growth. These practices foster resilience and a deeper appreciation for each step forward, enhancing one's ability to navigate both triumphs and tribulations.

Practicing gratitude involves acknowledging the goodness in life and recognizing the external sources contributing to this goodness, fostering both personal development and enriching interpersonal dynamics.

Concluding Thoughts

Reflection stands as a pivotal practice for anyone striving toward excellence, whether you are a young professional, mid-career individual, or entrepreneur. Throughout this chapter, we explored the important steps of assessing accomplishments and learning from past experiences. Recognizing milestones allows us to celebrate progress and builds a foundation for confidence in our abilities. Meanwhile, by examining challenges, we uncover lessons that refine problem-solving skills and bolster resilience. Documenting these experiences provides a continued narrative of growth, while feedback reflection introduces diverse perspectives that enrich personal development.

Adjusting goals based on current insights is another critical aspect highlighted in this chapter. As our lives evolve, so should our goals. This continual reassessment ensures that objectives remain aligned with our evolving priorities and values. Embracing the SMART framework offers clarity and precision in goal setting, providing a concrete path forward. By creating new challenges, we push beyond our comfort zones, fostering growth and innovation.

Moreover, maintaining a feedback loop fosters accountability and invites novel insights into our development journey. Together, these reflective practices equip individuals to adapt to change, drive personal and professional growth, and maintain momentum on the path to success.

Conclusion

In this journey together, we've traversed the landscapes of personal and professional development, navigating the principles that define true leadership and resilience. Each chapter has unfolded lessons aimed at empowering you to forge a path marked by integrity, purpose, and effectiveness. By reflecting on these insights, you're equipped not just to succeed in your current endeavors but to thrive as you continue to grow.

Our first steps took us through the crucial habits that lay the groundwork for excellence. We've delved into what it means to "Embrace the Foundation of Excellence," understanding that your journey begins with establishing solid core values. A commitment to such foundational values drives not just individual success, but inspires those around you. As we transitioned from one lesson to the next, embracing integrity and authenticity emerged as non-negotiable traits. Living truthfully, both within oneself and towards others, is what ultimately cultivates trust, a vital component in any successful endeavor or relationship.

Leadership, as we've explored, is not merely about directing others but involves a profound connection with one's own strengths and weaknesses. It's about listening more than speaking and leading with empathy. In today's dynamic, interconnected world, the emotionally intelligent leader stands out, making the emotional landscape as important to navigate as any business strategy or operational framework. Your ability to read, interpret, and respond appropriately to emotions—both yours and those of others—enhances teamwork, motivates colleagues, and can even transform organizational culture.

Beyond the internal work of self-awareness comes an external commitment: taking decisive actions that align with your vision. You've learned to set purposeful goals and create actionable plans. The challenges might seem daunting at times, yet each obstacle is another step toward honing your resilience. Celebrating every small victory fuels confidence and courage, enabling you to embrace life's complexities with grace and poise.

In this era, continuous learning and adaptability are keys to enduring relevance and competence. We discussed at length the need for lifelong education and self-improvement—skills essential for anyone wishing to remain at the forefront of their field. Whether through formal education, mentorship, or experiential learning, you have the tools at your disposal to stay informed and adaptive. One takeaway worth reiterating is the importance of stepping out of your comfort zone to learn new skills, take on different perspectives, and cultivate a mindset that embraces change.

Building relationships and fostering collaboration are no less significant. In fact, the power of a supportive community cannot be overstated. Humans are inherently social creatures, and success often involves collective effort—something we've explored through the principles of teamwork and synergy. By surrounding yourself with individuals who share similar values and aspirations, you enhance not only your experiences but also theirs. Sharing your struggles and victories leads to mutual growth, creating a network of encouragement and accountability.

As you reflect on the personal anecdotes and exercises we've shared across these chapters, I urge you to look inward. Which strategies resonate most with your current life stage? What principles can serve as catalysts for the transformation you seek? Remember, your professional journey is deeply intertwined with your personal growth. Embrace self-discipline as a powerful ally; it's in the daily decisions that your bigger-picture success is built, brick by brick.

The process of reflection is instrumental in aligning your present actions with future aspirations. Reflecting on past experiences offers insight into patterns of behavior that either drive success or hinder progress. With this newfound awareness, you're poised to make conscious choices that are congruent with your long-term objectives. Consider, too, the role gratitude plays in this equation— a grateful mindset fosters positivity, resilience, and contentment.

Stay curious, because curiosity is the seed of innovation and advancement. Maintain a thirst for knowledge and a willingness to adapt. Change is the only constant, and learning how to pivot gracefully can distinguish leaders from followers. Keep asking questions, keep seeking answers, and remain open to the endless possibilities that lie ahead. Surround yourself with diverse voices and perspectives that challenge your thinking and broaden your horizons.

In reflecting on the rich tapestry of love, we come to appreciate its profound impact on our emotional growth and social interactions. From the passionate flames of Eros that fuel romantic pursuits to the unconditional embrace of Agape that nurtures compassion, each type of love plays an integral role in shaping our experiences. The bonds of Philia highlight the significance of true friendship, while Pragma underscores the importances of lasting commitment, showcasing how love matures overtime. Moreover, we explored how Ludus embodies playful joy in romantic interactions, thriving on flirtation and spontaneity. This carefree love fosters attraction and deeper connections while allowing partners to explore without serious commitments. The self-love Philautia emphasizes self-care and compassion, nurturing well-being. It fosters emotional stability and empowers individuals to set boundaries, leading to healthier relationships and enriching connections with others. While Storge love represents deep affection found in familial and platonic relationships, emphasizing loyalty and companionship. This nurturing love creates security, trust, and a strong foundation for both friendships and romantic ties.

Additionally, recognizing the nuances of obsessive Mania serves as a cautionary tale, reminding us of the potential pitfalls in relationships. By delving into these diverse dimensions, we not only gain deeper insights into fostering healthier relationships but also empowers ourselves to create meaningful connections in every aspect of our lives-be it personal or professional. As we move forward, let us carry these lessons with us, fostering love in all its forms for a more fulfilling existence.

Moreover, don't forget the community aspect that thrives on connection and contribution. In the chapters discussing team dynamics, you've seen firsthand how collaboration can elevate outcomes far beyond individual efforts. Nurture your networks, lean on your colleagues, and be a beacon of support for others. The success that's shared creates a ripple effect, influencing countless lives and further reinforcing the importance of principled leadership.

Your story doesn't end here. This work is a starting point—one influence among many that will shape your life's narrative. As you move forward, it's your responsibility to apply these teachings with intention and grace. Continue to question, to strive, and to persevere, knowing that each day presents a fresh opportunity to refine your character and redefine your impact.

We invite you to deepen your understanding and enhance your experience by visiting the dedicated section of our website www.ruidasilva.org. Here, you'll find a treasure trove of resources designed to complement your reading, including engaging exercises, insightful blog posts, and the latest updates on our online and in-person courses. Explore our curated products and services that empower you to cultivate meaningful connections in your life.

Join our community and take the next step toward enriching your relationships today!

In conclusion, remember that the journey of becoming an Excellent Human Being is ongoing. It's an amalgamation of lessons learned, challenges overcome, and dreams achieved. Carry these insights forward with you—let them guide your endeavors, inform your decisions, and inspire you to uplift those around you. Here's to your success and the bright future you will undoubtedly create, fueled by the wisdom, courage, and determination you've embraced along the way.

www.ingramcontent.com/pod-product-compliance
Lightning Source LLC
Chambersburg PA
CBHW051134120626
46547CB00012B/795